Faith in Words

Faith in Words

A Celebration of Presbyterian Writers

Edited by Ann Weems and Louis B. Weeks

Geneva Press
Louisville, Kentucky

Scripture quotations, unless otherwise indicated, are from the New Revised Standard Version of the Bible, copyright © 1989 by the Division of Christian Education of the National Council of the Churches of Christ in the U.S.A., and used by permission.

Scripture quotations marked RSV are from the Revised Standard Version of the Bible, copyright © 1946, 1952, 1971, and 1973 by the Division of Christian Education of the National Council of the Churches of Christ in the U.S.A., and are used by permission.

See Acknowledgments, pp. vii–viii, for additional permission information.

Book design by Sharon Adams
Cover design by Eric Walljasper, Minneapolis, MN

First edition
Published by Geneva Press
Louisville, Kentucky

This book is printed on acid-free paper that meets the American National Standards Institute Z39.48 standard. ∞

PRINTED IN THE UNITED STATES OF AMERICA

04 05 06 07 08 09 10 11 12 13 — 10 9 8 7 6 5 4 3 2

Library of Congress Cataloging-in-Publication Data

Faith in words : a celebration of Presbyterian writers / edited by Ann
    Weems and Louis Weeks. — 1st ed.
        p. cm.
  Includes bibliographical references.
  ISBN 0-664-50170-2 (alk. paper)
    1. Christian literature, American. 2. Christian life—Presbyterian
authors. 3. Presbyterianism—Literary collections. I. Weems, Ann,
1934– II. Weeks, Louis, 1941–
PS509.C55F35 2004
810.8'38285—dc22

                              2004041163

Contents

Acknowledgments

"On Conjunctions and Other Meaningful Words," by Doris Betts, reprinted from *Christianity and Literature*, vol. 50, no. 2 (winter 2001). Originally presented as a speech on "Faith and Fiction" at the annual convention of the Modern Language Association in Washington, D.C., on December 28, 2000. Reprinted by permission.

Two stanzas of "Meaning" from *New and Collected Poems: 1931–2001* by Czeslaw Milosz. Copyright © 1988, 1991, 1995, 2001 by Czeslaw Milosz Royalties, Inc. Reprinted by permission of HarperCollins Publishers Inc. and the Wylie Agency, Inc.

"Acrimony and Friendship, and Unexpected Grace," by Vic Jameson; reprinted from *Presbyterian Survey*, October 1988. Reprinted by permission of *Presbyterian Survey* (now *Presbyterians Today*), 100 Witherspoon St., Louisville, KY 40202-1396.

"Grandfather's Prayers," by Marshall Jenkins, copyright 1993, Christian Century Foundation. Reprinted by permission from the May 10, 1993, issue of *The Christian Century*.

Subscriptions: $42/year (36 issues), from P.O. Box 378, Mt. Morris, IL 61054. 1-800-208-4097.

"Why Do You Write for Children?" by Katherine Paterson; reprinted from *Theology Today* 56, no. 4. Reprinted by permission of *Theology Today*.

"The Creation," from *God's Trombone*, by James Weldon Johnson, copyright 1927, The Viking Press, Inc., renewed © 1955 by Grace Nail Johnson. Used by permission of Viking Penguin, a division of Penguin Putnam Inc. Quoted in "We Are Earthlings," by John C. Purdy.

"Let's Not Be Afraid of Ambiguity," by Eva Stimson; reprinted from *Presbyterians Today*, May 1994. Reprinted with permission from *Presbyterians Today*, 100 Witherspoon St., Louisville, KY 40202–1396.

"Charity Begins at Homes with Lemonade Stands," by Bill Tammeus; reprinted by permission of *The Kansas City Star*, June 2, 2001.

"Putting the Amazing Back in Grace," in *Putting the Amazing Back in Grace*, by Ann Weems. ©1999 Ann Weems. Used by permission of Westminster John Knox Press.

Introduction

*R*eformed Christians in North America today live most often at noisy intersections. We inhabit intersections where arts and sciences meet faith. We worship God Almighty, who created the heavens, the earth, and fascinating arenas of understanding and endeavor. We follow Jesus Christ, once crucified at a wooden intersection. We work and play and support families and pray and care and vote and believe and doubt and sing and hope and lament and give and take—and do many of these simultaneously.

These crossroads engage the very heart of human creativity, challenge the best of human virtues to bring peace and justice hand in hand, and captivate the imaginations of the faithful. "Bible in one hand, newspaper in the other?" Karl Barth's succinct pronouncement on the equipment of the one to preach also described something of the needful things for each thoughtful Christian.

At these wonderful, clanging, and bustling intersections, traffic is frequently confusing, and sometimes wrecks occur. But we see the most interesting people, creatures, problems, and vehicles!

And writers of prose and poetry describing these intersections and all the rest of life give some special clarity to it and for it. An apt metaphor, a descriptive phrase that rings true, a character of a special scene or story—all these meaning-making works from people at the intersections help us navigate the ones we inhabit.

They also speak of other portions of God's creation—of pastoral and bucolic peace, of peoples long gone and of creation yet to come. They respond to some of the questions that arise from us at our intersections.

How do we translate the gospel, speak of faith adequately, perceive and describe God's benefits in our day? What words provoke us to discern and consider the grace of God? How do we hear profoundly our plight and possibilities as human beings?

In our day, people of faith speak creatively and beautifully of God's activity and our human condition. Christians who are Presbyterian may bring distinctive beliefs, distinguishable practices, and a peculiar culture to the table for that enterprise. Fiction and poetry present in compelling fashion responses to these questions and explorations of these topics. Doris Betts writes novels and essays. Katherine Paterson writes books for young people. J. Barrie Shepherd publishes poetry, and Kathleen Norris writes "spiritual geography."

These women and men, and others in the Presbyterian Writers Guild, do constructive theology every day. Through the Writers Guild, we encourage one another in expressing the faith. We also rejoice in and support new writers who join in phrasing the faith and exploring the mysteries of Christian reality. We believe that God calls us in each generation to employ the gifts of writing for the benefit of others. As a mark of its existence for a full generation, the Guild offers an opportunity to write and to read of faith and words.

We seek in this partnership between the Presbyterian Writers' Guild and Geneva Press to provide some examples of Presbyterians offering words about faith today.

We invited some distinguished writers and poets who are Presbyterian to contribute works for inclusion in this book of exempla. We also invited all other Presbyterians—those who have published some poetry or prose, those who have written but not published, and those who have sensed the call to write—to submit a poem or a work of prose for consideration.

We accepted essays, short stories, poems, and a few other works of fact or fiction. We wish space could have permitted us to accept more of the works. Some of the contributors characterize themselves as "Christian writers." More characterize themselves as "writers who are Christian." We made selections based on the beauty and truth of the words and frequently on the compelling nature of the faith represented.

We are deeply grateful to Davis Perkins, David Dobson, and all the team at Geneva Press who encouraged the Writers Guild in this project. We are also grateful to members of the Presbyterian Writers Guild who shared in planning this volume.

Gratefully,
Ann Weems
Louis Weeks

Table Grace

Jack Barden

*E*very Thanksgiving that we gather, which is becoming more and more rare these days, my family engages in what has been a ritual theological controversy for us for well over thirty years. A recent Thanksgiving holiday found me at my parents' home, a small gathering of forty or so extended family members and friends, some I hadn't seen in years, some I had never before met, all joined together for food and fellowship. I don't know about other families, but for my own, the holiday was anything but simple. There was tension and stress, as there always is when lots of people get together in one house, especially when they are all related. But amid the stress, there was also a sense of comfort, of familiarity, that exists among almost every family, even when brothers haven't spoken or parents are separated. Rituals common to our family were observed even if they went unnoticed. There was some bargaining about what football game would be watched when, and on which television. There was some time to tell the stories of childhood and family lore, as well as time to catch up on the little stories that make up our daily lives. And somewhere in the midst of all that, my family and I took time to pause for the traditional feast, and to give thanks.

As we stood, gathered before the meal, several people had something to say, things they were thankful for, memories of family and friends no longer with us. Then I was asked, as the only "professional pray-er" in the family, to say the blessing. That's when it began: after I said an appropriately pastoral prayer, everybody joined hands, and we said *it* together out loud. *It* is that blessing, you know the one; everybody knows it: "God is great, God is good. Let us thank him for our food. . . ." Growing up in my family, nothing was simple, not even a childhood prayer.

It goes back to when I was a small child. Like most well-meaning Christian parents, my parents taught their children to say grace before supper. So we learned that prayer:

> God is great, God is good.
> Let us thank him for our food.
> By his hands we all are fed.
> Give us, Lord, our daily bread.

We said that prayer before supper regularly for a few years. Then we found ourselves right in the middle of the early 1970s, and my mother's social consciousness was awakened. One evening, before supper, we began not with grace, but with a theological discussion. All people, my mother pointed out, are not always fed. Some people go hungry, some starve, while others have more than enough. Her point was well taken, and yet we struggled as children with our simple prayer. How could we in good faith say, "By his hands we all are fed," when we recognized that many children would go hungry that very night? Surely God was not the kind of God who would desire that some be hungry while others stuff themselves to excess? What could be done? How could we address God faithfully and yet with concern for those who did not have enough food?

My mother, being the poet and theologian she is, suggested a simple alteration to our prayer: We would change the word "fed" to "led." We could faithfully affirm that God leads us all, even the hungry children. So began our new ritual:

> God is great, God is good.
> Let us thank him for our food.
> By his hands we all are *led* (emphasis added of course,
> for we were merely children)
> Give us, Lord, our daily bread.

This seemed to satisfy our family. We felt as if we had solved a great injustice muttered by millions without a thought for the theological consequences of their simple prayer. At least our family would be socially aware.

Then we had supper at my grandparents' house one time. All my cousins were there. When it came time to say the blessing, we all joined hands and began:

> God is great, God is good.
> Let us thank him for our food.

Suddenly, in the middle of a simple table grace my brothers and sister and I all had a theological crisis. Here it comes, we thought. Do we say "fed" and go along with everybody else, even though we don't believe it, or do we say "led" and cause controversy at the dinner table, breaking open a subject we weren't quite sure how to handle? We only had a moment to decide and the word was upon us. Which would it be: theological compromise and family harmony or steadfastness of conviction and possible chaos? As we heard our cousins mumbling, "By his hands we all are fed," it came out, louder than we intended because we were nervous: "*led*." There, we had said it. The grown-ups faltered momentarily; there was an uncomfortable silence. Then we continued, "Give us, Lord, our daily bread. Amen." There was some nervous giggling and some confused glances from cousins who didn't know what had just happened. How could they know that they had just been cast into a theological whirlwind that would blow across the face of every family gathering for the rest of our lives?

We arrived at a compromise for future family gatherings: We would say a shortened version acceptable to all. The final two lines would be omitted, thus avoiding the tension caused by the reality of the gospel in our imperfect human hands. But, in private, my immediate family would continue to affirm God's guidance even for those whose basic human needs go unmet by an unbalanced and self-focused society. Of course, I didn't think all of this at the age of twelve or thirteen. For most of us, it just became a game, a test to see who would remember to say *led* instead of *fed*. It was something insightful to bring up when we had guests for dinner. It was only later as I grew older that I began to reflect more deeply on that simple childhood table prayer.

"God is great, God is good." It begins harmlessly enough. At first, as a very young child, I misapprehended this beginning and I thought this phrase referred to God's color: God was not black or white; instead, God was gray. But once I was old enough to understand the word was "great," I lost that powerful image of God's color—at least intellectually, because I have to confess that I still imagine that if God has a color, that color is some gentle shade of gray, like fog or a mourning dove. These two assertions, I later learned, that God is both great and good, are classic Reformed theology. God is the all-powerful sovereign Lord who, out of God's inherent goodness, creates this world and calls it good. In God's providence, all the bounty of creation is given for the benefit of us and all God's creatures. And so the next line, in classic Reformed manner, follows that we give thanks to God for God's great goodness and providence toward us, in the blessing of food for our table. It's what our national holiday of Thanksgiving is all about, after all: recognizing that all we have—the bountiful harvest, the fruits of labor, the blessings of freedom—all of it flows not from our own abilities, but from God's great goodness. John Calvin would have been proud to hear the thousands of families muttering these words.

But then comes that troublesome next line: "By his hands we all are fed." It's troublesome because there is some truth in it: It is true that all we have comes from God's hands. So all who are fed are indeed bound to recognized God's hand of providence. And yet what about those people who are not fed? Does that mean God doesn't want to feed them? Does God not care about them too? It's not a problem of theology, though, not really. It is a problem of stewardship. God does indeed provide for the needs of all people. We have the capacity to produce enough food in this nation alone to feed the entire population of the globe. But in our human greed and arrogance, we believe that we have some inalienable right to consume as much of the world's resources as we can possibly manage to seize. If we have more on our table on Thanksgiving Day than some families eat in a week, well, that is our right. After all, we worked hard, saved our pennies, lived a righteous life, while others didn't. All too often we do not see the responsibility we have for faithful stewardship of the bounty we have harvested. We easily and thoughtlessly thank God for our food, with no remorse or conscience for those around the globe who suffer for our excess. It is all too easy to affirm in a self-righteous tone that God has blessed us with resources to meet only our own needs and that we need not be concerned for the needs of others. Perhaps it is more appropriate to affirm that we recognize God's providence in leading us and all God's children to a right use of God's creation, rather than murmuring in prayer some self-aggrandizing assurance of our value to God equated with our possession of excess.

After all that, though, how can we in good faith petition God to give us our daily bread? Isn't that in direct conflict with the very same self-centeredness just altered in the preceding line of the simple childhood table grace? Perhaps it is

selfish of us if we come to God seeking daily bread because
we seek to fill our stomachs, just as the crowds sought out
Jesus for more bread because they had eaten their fill and
wanted more. But if we can honestly pray through the theological crisis of that former phrase, then we arrive at a
moment when we bow in uncomfortable silence before God.

In that silence our hearts whisper our selfishness. In that
silence our souls sigh of our sinfulness. In that moment of
silence we recognize how unjustly we have hoarded God's
bountiful gifts and we repent of our faithless stewardship. In
that time of silence we fervently pray that God in all of God's
goodness and greatness might forgive us and strengthen us to
reorder our lives so that we joyously and thankfully share
with others the blessings we have received.

And when we pass through that moment of silence, we
arrive on the other side, able to pray with conviction of faith,
"Give us, Lord, our daily bread." Then, our prayer is a prayer
of faithful stewardship that we desire no more than our share
of God's bounty. Then, our simple table grace becomes a confession to the world of our faith in a God who is both great
and good, a God who cares for all humanity, regardless of
their abilities to purchase or produce feasts of excess, a God
who knows our needs before we even ask and has graciously
sought us out and provided for us in justice and mercy. Then,
our prayer is a prayer of sincere response to the good news
we know in Jesus Christ. Jesus said to the crowd, "It is my
Father who gives you the true bread from heaven. For the
bread of God is that which comes down from heaven and
gives life to the world" (John 6:32–33). With the crowds, our
prayer is one of petition: "Lord, give us this bread." Jesus
said, "I am the bread of life. Whoever comes to me will never
be hungry, and whoever believes in me will never be thirsty"
(John 6:35). When we have struggled with the theological
crisis of table grace, then finally our prayer is a prayer for the
salvation of the world.

Lord, we come to you; satisfy the hunger of our hearts' desire. Lord, we believe in you; quench the thirst of our souls' longing. God, you are great, and God, you are good. And, Lord, we thank you for our food. By your hands, Lord, we all *are led*. Give us, Lord, our daily bread. Amen.

On Conjunctions and Other Meaningful Words

Doris Betts

Some of you may teach college writing, as I have for thirty-four years, the many kinds of writing spanning the spectrum from required freshman composition to advanced fiction workshops. And probably we all teach toward clarity and brevity; we will not today deal with Oscar Wilde's comment that St. Paul's prose style was one of the principal arguments against Christianity.

When evaluating essays, we teachers hope that our students have chosen specific, precise words after weaker words were discarded, working through several revisions until their final drafts have sifted wheat from chaff. Randall Jarrell once said that the purpose of his class in writing poetry was to help beginning poets perform such winnowing of words, that before taking Jarrell's course a student poet might find the right word after six or seven false starts—"But after you've taken my class? Maybe three or four."

In my story "The Ugliest Pilgrim," Violet realizes that she has all along misunderstood the name of Oral Roberts' headquarters building in Tulsa. She'd always thought he preached from the Hope AND Glory Building, only to find it's merely the Hope OF Glory. She says ruefully that you wouldn't think one little word could make that much difference.

8

After a lifetime of staying alert to many little words, I naturally note your conjunction, Christianity AND Literature, "and" being Violet's favorite conjunction. It's also a favorite in the Bible and with William Faulkner, joining units that have the same status or value. That word "and" must also be the only conjunction the average college freshman has ever heard. Max Steele often complains about the excessive use of "and" in early student stories, where it produces what he calls "baby sentences" that equalize unlikely and disparate events. For example, a child will give this report of his trip downtown: "I walked down Main Street and we ate ice cream and a truck ran over a man and killed him and I got to ride on the seesaw." Such leveled-out coordination with the word "and" could continue indefinitely.

But here, in joining Christianity AND Literature or Faith AND Fiction, the word makes a paradoxical pair and then shuts up. If it had been Christianity OR Literature, that would have reflected the prevailing outlook of those scholars who think that T. S. Eliot sold out in *Four Quartets,* that Flannery O'Connor's Catholicism cramped her talent, but that Graham Greene finally wised up.

You could have joined those big topics with prepositions: Christianity AGAINST Literature, FOR Literature, IN SPITE OF Literature. Before. Over. With. Instead Of. On Behalf Of. Each choice would have altered why we meet here today. Thomas Merton once feared he'd have to make that linkage using the word "or," in the early days when he thought "one of us, the poet OR the monk, must die."

Far better writers than I have stood before you making coordinate statements such as "I am a Christian, *and* I am a writer." Most of us prefer the word Christian as a noun the way Paul first used it at Antioch; we believe that the adjectival use, as in an ad for a Christian used-car dealer, should lead to widespread snapping shut of pocketbooks. There's a gas station in central North Carolina with a sign

out front that says: "WE TITHE. BUY GAS FOR JESUS."
I drive on by.

Madeline L'Engle drew her own distinction in this quotation: "A CHRISTIAN writer might want to mention the name
of Jesus a requisite number of times, or might omit a word or
scene that was ugly. A writer who IS a Christian might never
mention Jesus, and might write shocking words or incidents."
Like her, I believe that the surface of fiction can be secular
and still not block the light.

A secular surface can also mislead, however. It has gotten
Ms. L'Engle criticized by fellow Christians who haven't
found her writing Christian *enough.* Readers who admire the
poetry of Mrs. Billy Graham may not respond to Gerard
Manley Hopkins. The Holy Office condemned Greene's *The
Power and the Glory,* and Evelyn Waugh said that Greene
wrote mad blasphemy. Miguel de Unamuno was denounced
as a heretic.

Then there's the risk that what you thought was a secular *surface* has actually solidified all the way down. I teach
at Chapel Hill, a tax-supported university where church
and state can seem so widely separated that Evel Knievel
couldn't jump across. By not proselytizing in the classroom, I apparently give off no light at all. A low point came
when my Presbyterian preacher, by accident or perhaps to
divine amusement, happened to be seated on an airplane
next to one of my students. After their awkward do-you-
know conversation had dredged up my name, the preacher
said, "Oh yes, she's very active in our church," to which the
student blurted with utter amazement, "Mrs. BETTS???"
(It would have been charitable of him not to tell me, especially with so much relish.)

We live between the modern anxieties of too much or too
little: anxieties that we might become as lukewarm as the
church of Laodicea so God will spew us out of His mouth; or
that what we considered good balance has worsened into split

personality, half of which is ashamed of the Gospel of Jesus Christ; that a proper pedagogy prefers that *The Iliad* and other real literature offer no moral lessons. And, besides, nobody wants her appendix taken out by a surgeon who asks as he lifts his scalpel, "Are you saved?" The same implied question by an author lifting her pen also puts us off.

William Buckley has said that, if you mention God more than once at New York dinner parties, you aren't invited back. And the book reviewer who did the most sales harm to my last novel, *The Sharp Teeth of Love,* groaned in the *Washington Post* over its excessive religious content, though she did write one sentence that tickled me: "This novel reads as if its author had been kidnapped by a theologian on speed."

Even a writer who is active in her church may be just as active in the nearest library, where that word "and" still shimmers between Sundays and weekdays, between the Holy Book and books in general. Stories about the Prodigal Son and the lost sheep got me ready to read *King Lear,* where the weak and foolish characters also have greater value than the cunning and self-centered.

For many years, however, I chose the library OVER the ecclesia, literature OVER Christianity. So did Alice McDermott, who recently recalled being in graduate classes back when fiction was the only altar at which she was then willing to worship. She returned to the church by WAY of literature, shot like an arrow through Faulkner's well known Nobel Prize speech. In middle age, she says, "the questions I most wanted to ask as a novelist were the questions the Church had already given language to." She then adds, "What I wasn't prepared to discover, or to rediscover, was that they were questions for which the Church also provided answers."

Writers take me deeper into those questions and answers than most theologians (even theologians on speed!)—writers like Ron Hansen, André Dubus, W. H. Auden—but in recent years especially women writers, who have hiked through my same wilderness more likely carrying pen and ink in an apron pocket than rod and staff in hand.

Writers like Anne Lamott—in *Traveling Mercies* she's as radical a Christian as Jesus was. Or Nancy Mairs, who can get to God's love by way of multiple sclerosis and infidelity. Not since Hopkins has this natural world seemed as shot through with incandescent meaning as by Annie Dillard who, like most of us women, can only climb the heights of abstract theodicy from the bedside of one burned child. Dillard says that even as a girl she had a head for religious ideas: "They made other ideas seem mean." Or Kathleen Norris in her Dakota landscape no more verdant than Judea, who connects the discipline of Trappist monks with our daily, sluggish craft of writing. Both, she says, are not so much subjects to be mastered as ways of life that require continual conversion. Though both she and Denise Levertov rediscovered the value of the Psalms while staying in monasteries, both women are poets, not novelists; you remember that when Brocklehurst asked Jane Eyre what *she* liked best in the Bible, she chose those books with the most vivid, even violent, stories and added that "Psalms are not interesting."

Women writers are tough on the Old Testament. Faye Weldon takes the side of Delilah over Sampson; June Jordan rereads Ruth and Naomi with a new slant.

And on the subject of religion itself, women writers seem more good-humored than full-time theologians. In a novel by Rebecca Hill you get asked, "Are you a Bryl-Creme Christian? A little dab'll do ya? An Alka-Seltzer Baptist? Put him in the water and he'll fizz for half a minute? Are you a C&E Christian—Christmas and Easter?"

Lorna Kelly, in her memoir *So the Woman Went Her Way,* writes about meeting Mother Teresa for the first time. Taking a hard look at Kelly's glittering jewelry and bright red nail polish, the Mother told her to stop adorning herself in luxuries and to spend her money on the poor. Instantly Kelly replied, "That's exactly what Judas said to Jesus." After a moment of astonished silence, Mother Teresa burst out laughing.

That same New Testament story about a woman who wiped Jesus' feet with her hair has been summarized by Mary Gordon as "the triumph of the aesthetic over the moral." She selected another connecting word that chooses between, "aesthetic OVER moral," but I hear Mother Teresa's laughter as a wider, more inclusive choosing, one that accepts both the event and her own inconsistency and laughs. "Rejoice," Paul wrote, "and again I say, rejoice."

The words of these women writers speak to me partly because their thought processes are inductive more than deductive, but also because that conjunction "and" functions so strongly in the balancing act of all our female lives—as in Wife AND Mother, Home AND Career. John Gardner wrote that since "life IS all conjunctions, one damn thing after another," literature must move beyond making lists into subordination, since stories and plot deal with what leads to what. McDermott reached the point when it seemed first that her own life, and then all lives, began to have plot and not mere sequence.

I once heard a high-school English teacher talk about trying to motivate his teenage students, getting them as usual to write what they knew, but he had one notable failure. In a conference he attempted to draw out details about the boy's life, seeking potential subjects he could write about. "What about hobbies?" "No." "Or sports, do you play sports?" "Nope. Not good at sports." "Favorite school subjects?" He didn't like school. "Any extracurricular activities?" "Well, I play in the band." AHA, thought the teacher, GOT HIM! "The band! And what instrument do you play?" "Play the tuba." "Tuba! Fascinating! I don't know one thing about a tuba. Tell me about playing a tuba." "Not much to it." "No, no, help me understand the experience of making music on the tuba." "Well, you just blow in one end, and it comes out the other."

What became clear to the teacher as they struggled through this dialogue was that the student's life itself was impoverished precisely because he lacked the words to make its content interesting even to himself. Don't we all know someone who can retell an experience we've shared and recount it so vividly that the retelling becomes better than the event itself? My father was one of those improvers of reality. My mother said he'd rather climb a tree to tell a lie than stand on the ground and tell the truth.

The high-school teacher's point was that in the end all we have left of our lives are the words we used to tell ourselves about them. Whatever this audience or these readers were doing at 7:00 A.M. this morning is gone, except as you recall the moment in language. Words are the shining trail that stretches behind each one of us; words are the means of story; words produce the plots we impose on, or discover in, our lives.

Never has this been clearer to me than recently, when I've been forced to meditate on the conjunctions that link past AND present, body AND mind, life AND death.

My mother, now 89, has lived with us for some years in declining health, what L'Engle summarized so well as this "dwindling," until this spring when she became too heavy to lift from her frequent falls. She then moved into a facility two miles from our home, euphemistically overestimated as "Assisted Living," and there on 12 December she had a stroke. Her condition has since stabilized at a minimal level she would hate. In bed now she sometimes wakes, and her expression reveals that she has recognized me, or hasn't, and a few times she has spoken my name in a stranger's voice. Once she struggled to croak out "How's mama? How's granny?" Since they have been with God for more than fifty years, I was able to assure her that they were just fine.

Mostly I sit talking into her better ear, talking to the memory of her, talking with and to all the WORDS I know about her, for where is my real mother now? Has that conjunction "and" come permanently unhooked between her body and her mind? Would not a materialist insist that the mother to whom I continue to speak these unacknowledged words has always been a mere functioning of brain cells, the personality now erased by thrombosis, the remnant now mostly metabolic; and that even the story I know about her and even my anxiety are also no more than the whir of synapses near where my own thrombosis may already be stealthily taking shape?

I watch her sleep, thinking about the girl she was, a girl I can never know except imaginatively: poor, rural, born with a cleft palate, and humiliated by peers when the use of a drinking fountain would cause water to gush from her nose. A religious girl, who hoped that some day like Hannah she might bear a child who could speak words clearly, clear enough to go abroad and speak good news to the heathen.

Unfortunately, she only got me.

I have to admit that Mother has never been able to read any book of mine all the way through, that her idea of story comes from *Hurlbutt's Story of the Bible* and Dwight L. Moody's sermon illustrations. And these days, when I watch her mouth drop open and hear the snore begin, I remember how long she saved money from her cotton-mill job to send me to college, remember how only many years later could she save enough for her cleft-palate surgery. And how she phoned me after that operation to ask how she sounded with that lifelong nasal twang gone at last, and I—Fool! Fool!—blurted out that I preferred the familiar voice from my selfish childhood.

At our parents' bedsides, where we are all just overgrown children, we whisper the old prayers and the 23rd Psalm, but when we've later come out of the hospital into the thin winter sun, maybe we pair Scripture with a poem as well. I sometimes say the one, with which I will close, called "Meaning." It's by Czeslaw Milosz, who has previously been honored by the lifetime Achievement Award from the Modern Language Association. We met while he spent a semester at Chapel

Hill, and he gave me this poem in a broadside that hangs in our downstairs hall.

The first of three verses opens with confidence, saying that the speaker in the poem believes that "when I die I will at last understand the meaning of the world," that what is now incomprehensible will then be comprehended. But in the second verse the questions begin:

> And if there is no lining to the world?
> If a thrush on a branch is not a sign
> But just a thrush on the branch? If night and day
> Make no sense following each other?
> And on this earth there is nothing except this earth?
>
> Even if that is so, there will remain
> A word wakened by lips that perish,
> A tireless messenger who runs and runs
> Through interstellar fields, through the revolving galaxies.
> And calls out, protests, screams.

The God Journal

Donna Blackstock

God? My name is Kate Boyd. Did I need to tell you that? This is Marguerite's idea (if you already know this, stop me). She's my therapist. She says I have some issues with you and suggested I try writing you. So . . .

You can read over my shoulder. Or you can browse through this journal whenever you feel like it. If you'd like to write something back, maybe respond to something I've said, you go right ahead. I can hear Marguerite saying, "You're wasting God's time. Get to the point."

Right. God? I don't know if you're there or not. That is, I know you're there, that you exist; what I don't know is if you pay any attention to people. But if you do, I just have one question: What the hell are you doing?!?

❧❧❧❧❧❧❧

I visited my mother today. Remember her? Millicent Wexler? She's one of your staunchest supporters. Of course, I understand that doesn't mean much to you since you're an equal opportunity God and you don't want to show favoritism, which is good, except . . .

As far as nursing homes go, it ain't bad, which is good, because we can't afford anything better. Remember when

Mom used to visit that nursing home years ago? Maplewood Manor? That was a pitiful place, but she took it on as part of her ministry. (Did you know she had her own ministry? Do you *really* know our names and the number of hairs on our heads? It seems like a lot to keep track of. Then again, if anybody is likely to have a good data-processing system, it would be you.)

Maplewood Manor. First there was the smell: disinfectant, urine, old people decaying. The first few minutes I always felt like gagging. Then the sounds. The mumbling and muttering, the meaningless blather and blither, the rantings, sobs, the moaning. Then there was the grabbing. People lined the hallways, tied to their wheelchairs. They reached out to grab your hand, your arm, your leg, any piece of clothing. Stop. Hold my hand. Comfort me. Talk to me. Save me. Tell me who I am. As a child I found it frightening. But what frightened me more were the leftover bodies. The people who looked at you and never saw you, who looked straight through you like you didn't exist, the ones whose souls and minds had vacated and left behind their empty sacks of flesh and clattering bone. Mom loved them. She touched them and hugged them; she knew their names. She listened to them. She brought them little gifts: cookies, hankies, Easter eggs, companionship.

Mom dragged my brother, my sister, and me to Maplewood Manor every Christmas—it was traditional—and any other time we weren't quick enough with an excuse. Dad rarely went. He claimed the credit of visits to the nursing homes where his parishioners resided. You do remember Dad, don't you? Alan Wexler? Surely you have a roster of your priests. Dad used to say that he must be from the tribe of Levi, which explained (1) why he was a minister, and (2) why he wore jeans all the time.

One Christmas Mom dreamed up an instrumental presentation of carols for Maplewood Manor. David and Tam were in the marching bands at their schools. I was struggling to play the guitar, which I gave up soon thereafter. Mom played the piano. So we had Mom on piano, me on guitar, David on sax, and Tam on the bass drum. The Wexler Family Band, complete with Santa hats. We were incredibly bad. The aides rolled their eyes, but the patients seemed to appreciate us. They gathered around, wide-eyed, or at least awake. Some of them tried to sing along, which, with our uneven tempo, was impossible. Actually Tam kept the beat going, but I couldn't change chords fast enough. David got flustered by the audience and lost his place several times; when he resumed playing he rarely landed on the same bar as Mom.

A man with a cane shuffled toward us. His wispy hair hovered above rheumy eyes. All he wore were boxer shorts and a robe, which was tied at the waist but not closed. He tottered to the bass drum, stood opposite Tam, raised his cane, and began beating the drum in counterpoint. Tam faltered. I giggled. David sputtered into his sax, which bleated and honked. Tam glared at us, picked up the beat from Mom, who was unflappable, and kept going. So did the old man.

The following Christmases we stuck to caroling.

One day Mom mentioned her plans for us to take cookies to Maplewood Manor. We protested vigorously. We told her how much we loathed the place. She began reciting how it was a godsend for some people. "Would you like to live there?" I blurted. Mom's eyes probably said more than she intended. For the first time I understood that she disliked Maplewood Manor as much as we did, and that was why she went there. "Heavens no!" she said. "But most of those people don't have any family to care for them."

David, Tam, and I waited a moment before we made eye contact. We made a silent pact then, which we reaffirmed in later years: we would take care of our parents and see that they never got left in a nursing home.

Then we grew up and our parents grew old.

❧❧❧❧❧❧❧

Dad was lucky—at least in the death department. He died with his boots, and his Levis—on, fishing in the San Gabriel River. They found him in the water, his back against the bank and a trout on the line. The coroner said it was a heart attack. Dad wasn't so lucky in the life department. When I was about ten or so I asked Dad how come God didn't heal him. It seemed so simple to me then. The Bible says, "Seek and ye shall find; ask and it will be given unto you."

(God, I hope you don't take off points for misquotes, but I'm not looking it up. And I'll admit it: my memory's not what it used to be. Maybe you don't realize this about humans, but as we age some of our functions begin to deteriorate. Jesus only lived to be thirty-three, so he didn't have any firsthand experience with old age. That may be your problem right there. Since you did your incarnation-thing you think you understand what it's like to be human. Excuse me, but maybe you don't know the half of it.)

So anyway, I thought if Dad asked to be healed like Bartimaeus who was blind and that blind fellow in John, then of course you would heal him. Dad wasn't blind, but he was depressive. He always took care of his parish, though. While some of the parishioners may have known he fought depression, I doubt they knew how severe it was. But we knew. One of the things that depressed him and scared him most was that he doubted his faith.

Sometimes Dad thought he was a hypocrite and should leave the ministry. Sometimes he was afraid that he had spent his whole life serving a God who didn't exist. What a monumental waste that would be, not to mention all the people he had deceived with his false preaching. He wanted to believe. He loved you desperately, like a little boy who loves and yearns for the father who had deserted him. He loved you with all his heart and all his soul; it was his mind that harbored doubts. I think it was Mom who helped him forge the bridge between heart and mind, who kept his faith alive, who helped him hold on to it.

When I asked him why God didn't heal him, he said he fig-ured that you must like him pretty much the way he was. He said he was like the poster-boy for God, that if you could use him you could use anybody. He said he prayed to you con-stantly, and even confided his sign-off for his personal prayers: "Blessed be you, Almighty God. I am your humble servant. Help thou my unbelief."

Mom was your servant, too, I guess a more humble ser-vant because she received no validation for it. She wanted to be a minister, but when she was young and setting her life course women were not considered ordainable. So she did the next best thing, as they say, and married a minister. She spent her life serving others, behind the scenes, taken for granted. The church's notion of call bothered Mom. She thought it was contradictory for the church to preach to the laity about vocation when the only call it would recognize was the call to ordained ministry. She explained herself to me once, saying, "Many are called, but few are chosen. Many more serve, though they are neither called nor chosen. If I am doing God's will, God will bless my ministry. That will be my ordination."

Dick, my everlovin' husband, is worried about what I'm doing in this journal. He was brought up to be less secure in his relationship to you. He says, "Knowing you, Kate, you've probably bulldozed your way past disrespect and into blas-phemy." You scare him. You scare me, too, but in a different way. I try to calm him by explaining that you're big enough to take criticism and, in fact, seem to enjoy arguments from your lowly subjects. I remind him of Job, who wanted to take you to court but who could no longer afford a lawyer (thanks to you), and nobody was going to do pro bono work in a case against God. Poor Job had to do the job himself. Dick says, "That's probably where the saying came from." What saying?

I ask. He replies, "The one about a man being a fool who has himself for an attorney."

Job didn't really want to win, I tell Dick. It's like playing checkers with your father. You try to win a game off him from the time you're five until you're who-knows-how-old. Then one day you do it. You celebrate for one minute, and then you're devastated, because the world no longer seems like a dependable place.

Dick points to the journal. "So what do you want?" he asks.

ᘛᑎᘁᑎᘁᑎᘁ

Mom never did anything spectacular. Although she did invite the Boxlys to Thanksgiving four or five years running, something which the rest of us, Dad included, saw as a real test of Christian forbearance. Mrs. Boxly was a decrepit soul who lived on the edge of town in a small house on a large lot. Bobby Boxly, her son, was at least as old as our parents, and looked older. He was thin as ice in April. The love of his life was alcohol. When he moved back in with Mrs. Boxly, he dug up her yard and planted worms. He squandered just about every dime Mrs. Boxly had squirreled away for her old age, but the worm business brought in a little cash. The worms accommodated Bobby's drinking program; when he was up to it, he would dig for, or "pick," worms and sell the harvest to bait shops. He loved to talk about his worms at the dinner table. Mrs. Boxly with her spindly limbs and little potbelly reminded me of a spider. Through all the Thanksgiving dinners she moaned about her hardships, and though she complained about our cooking, she always asked if she could take some home.

The last time they came for Thanksgiving Bobby arrived, as usual, with a few drinks under his belt. We sat around in the living room trying to be hospitable while the turkey turned a fine bronze. Bobby went outside a couple of times "to check something on his truck." Then Mom put the bird on the table, and Dad said the blessing. Bobby stood up. "Excuse me a second, folks," he said, "but I gotta fire up the old truck again. The thermostat don't work right, and I gotta keep her warm."

"Sit down," said Dad.

"What?" said Bobby.

"You've had enough to drink. Please sit down and enjoy the dinner."

"No, sir," said Bobby. "Nobody tells me what to do."

"If you leave, you won't get back in," said Dad.

"Well now, that's nice, ain't it? Don't worry, mister, I won't be back."

He stepped toward the door, but Dad intercepted him and put a hand on his shoulder. "Give me the keys. You're in no condition to drive."

Bobby put up an argument about that, but finally Mrs. Boxly, who by this time had nearly finished her dinner, said, "He's right, Bobby. Give him the keys." Bobby cursed at his mother, which shocked us kids, but he dug into his pocket, slapped the keys in Dad's hand, and walked out.

Mom encouraged us to eat. We had been too goggle-eyed over the drama to think about food. Mrs. Boxly took a second helping of the candied yams. As she tipped them onto her plate she said, "There's another car key. It's in one of those magnetic boxes under the hood. He's gone."

When Mom drove Mrs. Boxly home that evening, the police were waiting for her. Bobby had smashed his truck and killed himself. Mom felt obliged to pick the worms. "I don't want you doing that!" Dad was furious. "And don't you even think about laying a guilt trip on me so I'll go pick them. I at least tried to save Bobby's miserable life, which is more than his mother did. It is beyond me why you think you should pick those damned worms." Mom had her reasons. Dad tried one more tactic: "Don't worms hibernate in the winter?"

"Oh sure," Mom said. "In Southern California?"

What all of us in the family knew about worms you could put on one hook. One day when we were waiting for Mom to come home, Dad said, "Your mother can't stand worms. That's why she won't fish. She doesn't want to touch the worms."

❦❦❦❦❦❦❦

Have you seen my mother lately? Look at her. She can't get out of bed. She doesn't know her name or mine, and I hope she's forgotten yours. Otherwise, she'd be wondering where you are. She can't express her thoughts or wishes or pains to us. She is trapped and isolated inside her body. Why have you designed us so that so many people have to endure such hellish aging? This woman has loved you with all of her being, and you condemn her to this tortured existence! Aw, what's the point?

❦❦❦❦❦❦❦

Mom died this morning. Please tell me you were with her at the end. Please tell me you have welcomed her home and given her a big hug. Please . . . please . . . please. . . .

Blessed be you, Almighty God.
I am your humble servant,

Kate

Help thou my unbelief.

"God Spoke the Word . . ."

Kathleen Long Bostrom

Before the time when time was kept,
The earth was empty, dark and deep.
Across the wrinkled waters swept
A mighty wind that knew no sleep.

Then in the chaos came a voice,
That made the darkness quake with fear;
Announcing God's creative choice
To organize the biosphere.

According to a holy plan,
God spoke the Word, and life began.

God spoke the Word—the Word was "light"—
And light there was from that time on.
With power to shatter dark of night,
Or gentle as unfolding dawn.

And in that light, God looked around,
And seeing what the Word had done,
God laughed, and filled the earth with sound:
Creation's song had just begun.

According to a holy plan,
God spoke the Word, and life began.

The words spilled forth in joyful praise
That then gave birth to lands and seas,
And plants and seeds and nights and days,
All kinds of creatures, birds, and trees.

And when the earth was all in place,
And seemingly all nice and neat,
God said, "There's still an empty space,
The world is somehow incomplete,
Until I make someone who shares
My precious gift of word and speech,
With whom I can converse in prayers,
Who uses words to bless and teach
(and sometimes, even, yes—to preach).

God gathered all the Trinity—
The three decided to consult.
Agreement came quite easily,
And people were the end result.

According to a holy plan,
God spoke the Word, and life began.

At first, they chose their words with care,
To name, to sing, to love, to bless.
But soon, instead of praise and prayer—
They chose their words to hurt, oppress.

They turned from God, and tried to hide,
And then it went from bad to worse;
They strangled truth, they cheated, lied,
And used their words to kill and curse.

And with their precious gift of breath,
Instead of life, their words brought death.

God watched the world grow dark and dim
As people sought to quench the light.
But when it seemed that all was grim,
God gave the people back their sight.

The Word which brought the world to birth
And molded chaos into form,
And shaped the heavens and the earth,
Into a silent night was born.

The Word became the blood and flesh
That burst to life in Bethlehem,
And Mary nursed in humble creche.
Creation's song was heard again.

According to a holy plan,
God spoke the Word, new life began.

The Word was full of truth and grace
That fed a world grown sick and sore,
And gave to God a human face,
That let the people hope once more.

In Christ, the words again became
The chorus of creation's song,
That healed the wounded, blind, and lame,
And let them know they all belonged.

But when Christ died upon the cross,
A silence spread across the land;
For with his death came such great loss,
There were no words to understand.

Three days passed by, and on the third,
God raised to life the living Word!

And in that act, God gave the gift
Of risen words to tell and bless,

Until all people hear, and lift
Their hearts to God, as tongues confess.

We tried to douse the light—and failed,
The Living Word of God prevailed.

Our words have power to create
A place of safety, refuge, trust;
Or they can give a voice to hate,
And leave a body broken, crushed.

Our words can cause the heart to sing,
Or cut the soul with verbal knife,
Or lift us up on eagle's wing,
And bind a wound, and give new life.

We bring to God with painful groans,
The broken pieces of our soul.
Though sticks and stones may break our bones,
The Word of God will make us whole.

All praise to Christ, the living Word,
The light for all the world to see;
The truth forever spoken, heard,
The only Word that sets us free.

Hallelujah! Amen

Butterflies

Patricia Bulko

Gentle as rainbows,
Kissed by the sun,
Soft as the moonbeams,
When each day is done,

Fluttering butterflies
Dance in the air,
And give me the feeling
That God's breath is there.

A Readiness Remembered

Stephen Doughty

Better than thirty years have passed since the summer I spent as their guest. Officially, I was their "Summer Student Pastor," but "guest" comes much closer to the reality. They provided me with lodging, more food than I could eat, and more encouragement than I merited. Though my stated duty was to instruct and guide them, it was ultimately they, the entire congregation, who instructed and guided me. I suspect some of them knew all along that it would be this way.

Certain basics of their life stood firmly in my mind before I ever arrived in town. Their church, nestled in New England's Green Mountains, shut down in the winter. The congregation could not afford a year-round pastor. All they were able to manage was, for the summer, a seminary student with my level of experience (none) and then lay preachers into the fall. After the lay preachers came freezing weather and heating bills that, even in the 1960s, were too high to pay. The congregation itself would, I understood, be an unusual mix: well-off summer folk from the suburbs and cities of southern New England plus year-round residents who eked out their livelihood doing whatever they could.

"You'll find good, solid folk," I was told. The denominational official who said that spoke like he meant it. So this much I knew when I went there: good people; a somewhat unusual blend; a church open for worship part of the year; a congregation willing to take on someone, well, like myself. These things I held in mind, along with considerable excitement about the chance to be out of the classroom and on my own.

What I did not know was the rich gift that would come through this body of persons. That arose from the congregation over the next ten weeks and has continued to press itself upon me in all the years since. It came not in one way but in many. As I revisit it in my mind, I still find it too full, too ample to be defined by any single incident. And yet for all the different angles from which I have viewed the gift over the years, I am finding now it comes to sharpest focus in the gentle interplay between a stump sitter, a man who lay down his tools, and a widening circle.

The Stump Sitter

Let me start with the fellow who knew how to sit on stumps. He was only nine years old but had already become something of a prodigy at it.

My assigned dwelling for the summer was with two older women in the community. The first morning I did what I continued to do through the rest of the summer. I jogged down their driveway, along the dirt road running through the center of town and up toward the church. And it just so happened that there he was on a stump out in front of his house, not far from the church. He was small, blond, barefoot. I waved. He sat as motionless as the stump itself, except that he turned his head slightly to watch this strange bit of business scurrying past.

The same thing happened the next morning. I jogged and waved; he watched. And so on the next morning, and the next.

Unknown to me, though, something was building and on the fifth morning it broke. As I approached his stump, the young fellow suddenly thrust an arm forward, pointed sharply at me, and called out, "You! Before this summer is over I'm going to teach you how to sit on a stump!" The slightest hint of a smile broke around the corners of his mouth. I nodded, smiled back, and kept on jogging.

When I got inside the church office certain images started to move through my mind. They were of the self-flattering type: "Young minister befriends neighborhood child"; "Young minister sits on stump."

The sad truth, however, is that I never took the boy up on his offer. We became friends. We laughed. We talked as much as his shyness and my awkwardness would allow. But alas, not once did I say, "How *do* you sit on a stump?" and then go ahead, receive of his expertise, and just sit for however long he felt a novice could take it.

The omission was my loss. I have no idea where this person is now. He must be about to charge into middle age, if that is the proper way to put it. I was middle-aged myself before I even realized he was on to something I much needed to learn. Wherever he is, I am sure he is still way out in front of me.

The Man Who Lay Down His Tools

It was midsummer now. As I recall, he not only put down the hammer he was using. He unbuckled the belt that held all manner of other tools tight about his waist. He lay the belt on his workbench and took seven or eight steps directly toward me.

Half an hour before I had been in the office at the church. A knock came on the door. It was one of the summer residents, a jolly woman who, it had turned out, was aunt to a friend of mine in seminary. We had laughed at the discovery, and at tales of seminary, and at tales she told me of her nephew. Her face now was drawn.

"Steve," she said in direct and measured tones, "we just had a call from your parents. Your grandmother has had a stroke. It's not good. Your mother and father are driving on from Chicago. They said you would want to know. They thought maybe you would want to be there too."

My grandmother lived in western Massachusetts. We had eaten dinner together every Sunday all four years I was in college. The whole family had gathered for her ninetieth birthday just six weeks before. When the cake, with ninety candles on it, caught fire, she had laughed harder than any of us.

Yes. In my parents' words, I "wanted to be there too."

I thanked my new friend for telling me. I went outside, got in my car, and drove off to ask the chair of the congregation if I might have some time away. He was a carpenter, a year-round resident, and right now he was building an addition on the home of a summer family.

"Ed." I spoke his name through the open walls of the addition. The sun was bright and shown on his white hair. Normally he would have turned, smiled, given a few more licks with the hammer, or finished sawing a board.

"Ed." I am sure I only said his name once and not very loud. He looked directly at me. Then, without hesitation, he put down the hammer, lay aside his tool belt, and walked directly toward me.

After my explanation of why I was there, words followed from him. Kind words. I certainly could have time away, as much as I needed. Don't worry about Sunday. "Don't even think about it!" He would take care of the worship. Please, though, just let them know how matters were coming.

His words freed me to go. Some days later, when I returned from the memorial service for my grandmother, the warmth of the welcome I received lifted me. What I remember most, though, is a solitary image: on hearing the tone of my voice, and after a single look at my face, he lay down his tools so that he could be completely there . . . for me.

A Widening Circle

The widening circle was at first harder for me to perceive. What I was experiencing, so up front and easy to spot, was a readiness of spirit aimed directly at me. It met me from all ages and all angles. It saw, and gently chided, my too swift pace. It took time with my grief. It spread meals before me day after day in almost more homes than I could number. It encouraged me to take time off when I needed it. And always this readiness of spirit came through the flesh and blood particulars of one or another person's sensitivity, humor, gift of time.

As weeks passed, though, I realized that the availability shown to my needs was only a hint of what was going on. "Do you know what John does?" a congregation member asked me one day. I had no notion, except I knew that John, nearly seventy and a year-round resident, earned a small amount of money digging graves in the cemetery on the edge of town. The questioner explained. John, with what little he had, would periodically give to others in the community who had even less. And on those occasions when he dug a grave and a family stood about grieving, with no clergy to help and no sense themselves of what to do, John would gently come forward and offer to pray with them. He was, I gathered, never refused.

Two summer residents with a lovely lakefront cottage noted the number of young children in the area who had never received instructions in swimming or even in basic water safety. They took safety lessons themselves, and then for fifteen days opened their normally quiet residence to the dusty, then dripping bodies of children who came to learn, splash, swim along the shore.

On a ridge overlooking the town lay a summer camp for children with Down syndrome. It had come into operation recently, and contact between the camp and town remained minimal. This particular year, congregation members determined to welcome the camp more fully into the community. Soon afterward three pews in the church filled, each Sunday now, with campers and their young adult counselors. Stating an obvious reality, but one that much needed to be named, a member of the congregation noted, "This is doing something for us." As barriers of awkwardness faded and closeness grew, the hospitality was clearly doing something for everybody.

The list of caring actions could continue here, but ultimately it was not so much the list of deeds as something else that so impressed me. I began to sense that I occupied a small point on what was a very wide circle of caring. The circle itself was formed by the members of that congregation, looking outward, sensing need, responding to a hurt, a loss, a sudden joy. Whenever one or another of the group responded, the circle grew. The love widened. And those of us touched by the love became points along the circle. Touched, and then drawn in, we ourselves became more aware of the love as it grew.

After ten weeks, I packed the car and drove off for another year at seminary. Classes were starting up. That began to excite me, as did my ever-present hopes of rekindling a rather stagnant social life. Even so, I sensed that something had changed within me or, more accurately, that something had been planted within me by that good and caring body of people. Though I was not able to articulate it at the time, I had come as a mendicant, a spiritual beggar to their door. They had taken me in, tended to my needs, borne witness with their way of being, and then sent me forth with lessons for a lifetime.

When now I am too much in haste, a small child still points at me from a stump. When I am in need, or when I must set aside my own preoccupations to tend to the needs of another, I still see Ed instantly lay down his hammer and belt full of tools. When, amid all the confusion besetting congregations today, I strain for a clearer vision of what our communities of faith are to be about, I see again that widening circle of responsive love.

Readiness. Responsiveness to the lives and needs before them. As a community in Christ, this was their gift. Three decades, and the memory nourishes still. . . .

Jairus's Daughter and Our Son

Joan Ellison

I always loved the story of Jairus's little daughter and how she was brought back to life after her untimely death. I can imagine how she played during those hot days of sun and sand; how she ran and laughed with her friends; how she helped her mother; until one day she fell to her bed very ill. No cool water fresh from the well helped her parched tongue. No cool cloth on her feverish forehead relieved her burning flesh. Soon she slept as in a coma, her breath shallow and her body limp. Helplessly her family struggled to revive this precious child, their only child.

Then it was that Jesus' name was mentioned. Jesus was a healer. Everyone knew of his special touch, his care for others, his penetrating eyes, his words. Whoever he was, Jesus was their only hope. Someone must reach this man and bring him to the sickbed. Jairus ran quickly. He was well known. Jesus surely will come immediately to help his daughter, his only child.

However, time and distance, along with the heavy, milling crowd, intervened. There were people everywhere . . . striving, starving, curious humanity; a mob-like scene to be cared for first. No urgent request could disperse the congested streets where Jesus was surrounded. The way ahead leading to Jairus's house was cut off.

Jairus had reached his goal. The message had been delivered to Jesus' ears, but the delay was unavoidable. Time was at a premium, and the hourglass had run out. Soon another came running to announce that it was too late. Jairus's little daughter had died.

O, the grief and helpless, human sadness; the disappointment, the anger with delay. What now could be done? But the story continues. Following that critical race for healing there came an ending beyond human belief, and this was what fascinated me as a child. In the next scene we hear Jesus' words of hope and well-being: "The child is not dead. She is just asleep." Then laughter of derision ensued, mixed with loud weeping of everyone gathered. Jesus did not hesitate. He took her by the hand and said, "Child, get up"(Luke 8:49–55). His infinite kindness and mercy reached her heart and she responded. What a day! It was a happy-ever-after story that we still read even these many centuries later. Jesus brought a child back to life and health. Such unspeakable joy!

This ancient Bible story touched me as a child, and I've remembered it throughout my entire life. No need to attempt to explain it or question it. No need for anything but wondering and rejoicing. My faith was sure and secure. This story told of a miracle. Jesus healed. He was God's son and our savior. Odd how this girl remained nameless, known only as Jairus's daughter. But I can accept this and other healing, miraculous wonders Jesus performed. I believed. I can never explain it but I believed.

The Bible story of Jairus's only daughter and her miraculous healing, however, is not finished. This story has become a parallel narrative and daily grows more vivid in my memory because of our son, Andrew. So it was that a strange paradox happened. A startling similarity to the above story began to take place when our young son was diagnosed with leukemia when he was four years old. Our dear youngest son, our fourth child, was terminally ill with acute leukemia. Could a miracle happen to cure him? We would do all humanly possible to care for him. We were relatively young and naive enough to believe a cure was inevitable. I longed to send for Jesus to heal our son. The doctors said he could live three to five years. These were excellent physicians, eminent hematologists who had access to the most recent drug therapy in the United States. We had three older children, and all of us felt confident that a cure for this dread disease was "just around the corner." Our naïveté gave us hope. We believed. We coped. We decided within our family to each live as normally as possible and not let our son see us grieve and make him become anxious.

Our lives were in limbo. The news jarred us and wrenched our souls. Our hearts were broken. Our gut feelings were seared with pain, anxiety, and acute helplessness. Yet life had to go on, and during the next three years our hope waxed and waned. For three years Drew had been in and out of remission and in and out of hospitals. At times we even believed he was well. But the leukemia always struck again. Like a flood it kept inching closer, making headway even through the sandbags of the finest medical care.

People tried to help with physical encouragement. Our family life went on. Trip after trip to the doctors continued. Along the way we vacillated between cheerful hope and helpless grief. We tried to keep our faith viable and green, and in reality, our faith did mature. But very often it felt more like a grain of mustard seed. A faith utterly minute, tried and found wanting. How sure and secure we tried to be for others until they came to believe that we were "strong" and that we were "doing great." If we let down our false pretenses, the dam of tears would drown our struggling hearts. Thus it was that we continued for three years.

In the meanwhile, Drew somehow learned to read at a very young age. How and when I have no recollection, but he learned to read quite well, and by the time he reached the age of five, books had become his ally. Wherever he went he took along a stack of library books, and his superior reading ability seemed to help alleviate the pain and ever-present suffering. He read while riding in the car, waiting in doctors' offices, lying in the hospital. He enjoyed this beautiful talent, and it became a blessing both for him and for us as we observed. We became amazed at his intelligence and his patience. Never did he cry or fuss about taking the large number of pills each day. Week after week he stoically endured numerous blood samples taken and seemed to understand how essential this was for his recovery.

Yet all the while, never could I bring myself to discuss his illness with him. . . . "We never spoke of death/my son and I/his young life seemed immortal/he could not die/grow cold/cease play/stop living/decay." Yes, in retrospect, I was in a state of denial. I could not speak of the prognosis to anyone. . . . "We never spoke of death/We played a game/his illness grave and terminal/deserved no name/he could not die/doctors/drugs/a miracle/my heart cried. . . . We never spoke of death/he was too young to understand/I rationalized/yet all the while we knew/it was to come/he, more than I/sought reasons/needed answers/to questions/some reply/ We never spoke of death/yet he did die/his pain-filled life snuffed out/no more to suffer/laugh or shout/reach manhood/realize talents/ believe or doubt/We never spoke of death/yet he did die/agonized his final breath/ah yes/and how deeply I regret/that while he lived/we never spoke of death."

How deeply I do regret this omission and often wonder what innocent or wise insight Drew may have shared, had I faced the issue of death with him. I evaded the topic for the simple reason that I was unable to talk about it without breaking down in tears. How far better would it have been, in retrospect, had we let him see our loving tears on his behalf. I am sure that he knew, and I wonder if he thought perhaps we didn't care.

Unlike in the story of the healing of Jairus's daughter, our little son died. He was only seven. Much has been written about how unnatural it is to lose a child; to have one's offspring precede us in death. A parent, by all statistics and rights, should normally go first. Yet children, from the stillborn, to age seven, to a teenager, even to middle age or longer, all wrench our very soul when they die first. Never do parents want to give up a dearest child of any age. Never do parents think we have had them long enough. Never do parents want our dreams and plans for our child to be snuffed out prematurely.

So it came to pass on that last Sunday morning when Drew went to church, he took along his faithful book. He liked to read during the service. It helped him in ways unknown. Later that same afternoon we again had to rush him to the hospital, where he continued his heroic struggle for life but to no avail. After three years he finally was released from his long months of pain and brave suffering. He died that night.

It was only afterward that I noticed the story that Drew had been avidly reading in church. It was in a junior church school book, and the last story he had read before he died was the one about Jesus healing Jairus's little daughter. My wounded, grief-stricken heart had to smile at this strange coincidence. What a paradox. I will always wonder how Drew related to this story and if he may have considered that a miraculous cure for leukemia could happen to him. I feel sure that Jesus knew his name and that with his last breath on earth our little son finally saw Jesus coming to meet him and to heal him.

My faith assures me that our son, Andrew, now is healed and safe with Jesus. As King David said (2 Sam. 12:23) when he lost his baby son and was overcome with grief and remorse: "I shall go to him, but he will not return to me."

Out of, in, and into Eternity
(On Occasion of Ordination)

Elsie Gilmore

I have been touched by the Lord:

She formed me with her hands,
    Male and female in her image;
She gave me all that is needed,
    The garden for our pleasure;
She chose me because of my ordinariness,
    Sarai into a strange land;
She blessed me in spite of my lies,
    Rebekah in scheming trickery;
She kneaded me through forced labor,
    Jochebed in slavery;
She danced with me in anticipation,
    Miriam with her tambourine;
She called me to liberation,
    Rahab without a country;
She appointed me governor and judge,
    Deborah under a palm tree;
She ripped apart my conceit,
    Gomer in captivity—

She mended me in Bethlehem,
She taught me with simple stories,
She stood in my way when I wandered,

She washed my feet,
She endured my ridicule and slaughter,
She transcended my most powerful assault;

She claimed me as her own,
   Mary Magdalene in the garden;
She scattered me to the ends of the earth,
   Priscilla to another city;
She molded me in persecution,
   Teresa before her accusers;
She strengthened me in solitude,
   Coretta in her aloneness;
She nurtured me in community,
   Margaret in the company of God's people;
She laid her hand on my head:

I have been touched by the Lord.

A March for Justice

George W. Gunn

"*H*ow shall we sing the Lord's song in a strange land?" asked disheartened captives in Babylon in Isaiah's time. A kinship in spirit has drawn together exiles in every century, exiles all, separated from their dreams, their hopes, and their heart's desires.

Here, in the first years of the twenty-first century the struggle continues, with echoes of the voices and marching feet of previous generations. A generation ago freedom marchers sang "We shall overcome," and all the peace marchers were saying and singing was "Give peace a chance."

The center point of my several ministries in higher education came in the late 1960s when American students fell out of step with their times, and when the beat of a distant drummer shook them out of their apathy and moved them from their home states and campuses to the streets of the nation's capital.

Two singular events mark my own pilgrimage in that decade, each a march for justice.

In the early '60s I made a chapel talk at Austin College in Sherman, Texas, in which I asked these silent generation students, "When are you going to get to the streets and join your brothers and sisters in other parts of the world to protest injustice?"

It would be a mistake to suggest that my words started a revolution, for mine was but one voice, encouraging political action by college students, and discontent with the "silent generation" label. It was a malaise that was soon to surface during these fabled '60s. The conscience of the nation was being stirred as the United States became entangled in the conflict in Southeast Asia, and at home in the open advocacy of desegregation and civil rights.

By 1968, "The Movement" was under way. It was, clearly, a case of hearing a different drummer, and then stepping to the music—music at first heard as distant and then close at hand. It was time to march and to demonstrate the depth of newfound convictions, convictions destined to touch the conscience of the nation and to change, for their generation, the image of students as leading an ivy-towered existence. Freedom rides and lunch counter sit-ins had put students on the front lines of protest and in the headlines of the daily press.

For decades campus ministers related to the Presbyterian Church U.S. came to the Montreat Conference Center in Western North Carolina for an annual gathering. It was to Montreat that I returned in the summer of 1968. I was in campus ministry at the University of Arkansas and was an elected commissioner to the Presbyterian Church U.S. General Assembly meeting at Montreat. As I traveled with my family from Arkansas to North Carolina, Senator Robert Kennedy was gunned down in Los Angeles as he sought his party's presidential nomination. I read the startling news in headlines across a crowded restaurant in Knoxville. Only two months earlier Martin Luther King Jr. had died, assassinated in Memphis as he prepared to march with striking garbage workers, seeking justice.

In the heat of the summer, the disfranchised poor and minorities had camped out near the Lincoln Memorial in Washington, D.C., to dramatize their plight to a government reluctant to give priority to the domestic needs of its people. This was "Resurrection City," a city of tents and plywood shacks. Its alternating muddy and dusty grounds stood in stark contrast to the classic buildings and monuments nearby. Here, on the Mall, a Solidarity Day rally was scheduled, with an invitation issued to churches and other advocacy groups to join in a Poor People's March, to demonstrate solidarity with the poor.

The General Assembly meeting in Montreat had before it an overture in support of the Poor People's March, asking for official participation. The Presbyterian Church U.S. was the church body that had spoken out boldly in 1954, before the school desegregation ruling, to call segregation a sin and to call the church to repentance. To side with the minorities seeking economic justice seemed to me timely and an appropriate and faithful response by the denomination's highest church court.

I remember the plea of Bill Jones, a black minister from Jackson, Mississippi, who stood on the floor of the Assembly and warned that if we failed to support this cause, "I must go back home and tell my people that the church has turned its back on them." An affirmative action at this time, however, was not to happen. As a minister commissioner to the Assembly, I participated in the debate over official participation in the March, and I felt the pang of defeat and the burden of regret when the resolution lost by a 2 to 1 margin.

Then a remarkable thing happened. According to the parliamentary procedures of the General Assembly, those voting might have their vote recorded by name in the minutes of the meeting. I rose to my feet and was recognized by the Moderator, Dr. P. D. Miller. I asked for confirmation of this right and received it, with the instruction to come forward to the

Stated Clerk's desk to register my dissent from the action just taken.

I moved into the aisle of Anderson Auditorium and walked toward the front. As I reached the Clerk's desk, I turned and looked back to see all four aisles filling with dissenters, coming forward. By signing our names, over one hundred of us voiced our personal support of the Poor People's March. The Moderator, on viewing the unexpected disruption of the agenda, declared a ten-minute recess.

The next day the *Charlotte Observer*, reporting on the Assembly in progress, had a headline that read "Poor People's March Begins at Montreat."

The next week most of the one hundred "Southern" Presbyterians marched again, joined by thousands of fellow Presbyterians and other people of faith. We gathered early for worship at the New York Avenue Presbyterian Church and moved on to the Mall, resolute in our call to identify with the nation's poor. From our vantage point on the steps of the Lincoln Memorial, I could see the face of the Great Emancipator to my right, and to my left, in the bright summer sun, a sweaty throng of black, brown, and white faces. A cardboard cap with a visor shaded the face of a young woman at my side. She carried no sign, but her eyes declared the message printed across her cap: "I have a dream." She stood only a few feet from where Martin Luther King Jr. first uttered those words, five years earlier.

It was 100,000 who sang and 200,000 hands clapped to celebrate the memory of slain heroes and the shared hope that "we shall overcome." As the shadows stretched long across the Mall, dusty demonstrators and drooping signs disappeared, swallowed up by Resurrection City, Trailway buses, and the suburbs of D.C. The visible unity and goodwill of that day was a high point of that tumultuous year—1968.

My fourteen-year-old son, Herb, and his sixteen-year-old brother, Wilson, who worshiped and walked with me that day, attribute the sharpening of their social conscience, and the awakening of their faith, to that experience, shared on a hot day in June in the midst of the civil rights movement.

The year 1968 had seen the assassinations of Martin Luther King Jr. and Robert Kennedy. In November, Richard Nixon defeated Hubert Humphrey for the presidency with the promise to end the war in Vietnam. With each passing month, however, the war expanded, the daily body count grew, and promises of peace went unkept. The fall of 1969 turned into a winter of discontent. A demonstration of anti-war sentiment, organized by a coalition of peace-advocating organizations, was scheduled for a November Saturday. Its centerpiece was to be a weeklong candlelight march past the White House.

I flew into Washington National Airport. In the gathering darkness I glimpsed the marchers from the air. From a spot north of the Pentagon, a single line of flickering lights filed across the Potomac River bridge and up barricaded streets past the White House.

Back in Arkansas two Little Rock ministers, Wellford Hobbie and Guy Delaney, had paid for a billboard on a main thoroughfare to speak their peace. It featured a red sun setting and this poignant message: "One more Son down in Vietnam is one too many." A weekly peace vigil had become the focus of antiwar sentiment at the University of Arkansas at Fayetteville. There, "The Deep End" coffee house embraced pro and con viewpoints throughout that fateful fall.

In Washington that night in November, I joined students from Arkansas and thousands of fellow protesters, "peace marchers," young and old, who gathered in a staging area, with Arlington Cemetery at our backs and the lighted monuments on the horizon. It was a solemn assemblage. Few words passed between us. The vapor of our breath drifted in the cold night air and warmed us, as we shivered in anticipation.

A single-file line had moved past this point for five days and nights. Our feet already numb with cold, our gloved hands took a lighted candle and a name. On a 3-by-10-inch card there was printed the name of one member of the military who had died in Vietnam. Wearing this name, we were instructed to march in silence and, when we reached the White House, to shout out the name we wore.

These names were circulated from the end of the march route back to the start, where they were stacked and reassigned, constantly and indiscriminately. Thus, what happened next took me completely by surprise and left me emotionally overwhelmed. The card handed me to hang around my neck bore the name "Charley Gunn—Texas."

I have a brother named Charlie Gunn, a medical doctor in Winston-Salem. It was a nearly impossible coincidence, but a circumstance I viewed as a gift, an act of grace. As I continued my journey across the bridge, I decided on a departure from the prescribed ritual. The line of marchers moved into the night. Ahead of me the voiced names grew louder, a roll call of the dead. As I reached a point opposite the White House, I held my candle high and shouted out with all the volume and intensity I could muster, "My brother, Charley Gunn!"

Hundreds of us gathered later that evening in the Washington Cathedral to worship and to celebrate our faith in the God whose will is our peace. One of the four featured speakers was a student from the University of Arkansas. Donna's husband was in Vietnam, drafted out of seminary because he would not accept a classification that would have kept him in graduate school. Once again we were saying and singing, "Give peace a chance."

The city was filled with anticipation but also anger. Tear gas floated toward us from DuPont Circle, where a noisy crowd was dispersed. The next morning buses of the marchers were parked, strategically, by the police to form a barrier between the streets and the White House grounds. President Nixon, we were told, watched football on television while a half million of his loyal subjects took their cause to the streets.

The faces on the platform near the Washington Monument were distant, but the words were familiar and the rhetoric echoed a common refrain, one sounded across the land, as the march toward justice gained ground and the conscience of the nation weighed its options. We were part of a movement toward a more humane and whole existence. We were sharing in rituals common to every generation, rituals that are renewed whenever the human spirit is moved to resist bondage, the compromise of its values, and is moved to celebrate its liberation. We were learning to sing the Lord's song in a strange land.

Returning to Washington in recent years, and to the Vietnam Memorial, I have stood silent before that awesome granite memorial and traced Charley Gunn's name with a trembling finger. I am moved to remember, with gratitude, those who went where duty called them, and those too who sought justice in another court.

Humbled, I meditate upon the universal qualities of love and of patriotism, the demands of which divided the nation, but qualities that, embraced, demonstrate a truth learned and needing to be learned again: with all the diversity of our convictions, in the end, we are brothers and sisters to one another.

Divine Service

Jeanette Hardage

There it was—
an impossible cleanup job
accomplished.

I more than tithed the Waiter.
Still, it hardly seemed enough
for service beyond
all reasonable hope.

The Situation Is Hopeless but Not Serious

James R. Hine

*W*hy not use a title that appears to be a more optimistic way of looking at life and say: The situation is serious but not hopeless? It certainly would be appropriate to make that approach. But let us turn it around and think about this: The situation is hopeless, but not serious.

Why pick this approach? Many years ago I attended a seminar conducted by Paul Watzlawick, who at the time was clinical associate professor of psychiatry, Stanford Medical Center.[1] He reinforced a number of questions that often came to my mind as I lived my life and conducted my counseling and ministry: Why do people let the guilt and anger of the past injure their lives? Why do so many live by the myth that promises the search for happiness will eventually lead to happiness? And why do people look for right solutions in the wrong places? In 1983 Dr. Watzlawick elaborated on these questions in a book titled, *The Situation is Hopeless, but Not Serious*. The subtitle of his book is *The Pursuit of Unhappiness*.[2] In it he explores the matter of how we are able to turn ourselves into our own worst enemies. By using the word *hopeless*, I believe Dr. Watzlawick to mean that some behavioral patterns lead to disaster unless there is a radical change.

Many people make themselves miserable about circumstances over which they have no control or events no longer available for change. If Christians would take chapter 6 of Matthew seriously, they would find a resolution of these problems to be rather clear. They would learn that in many cases, though the situation seems hopeless, it is not serious. And though the situation *is* hopeless, a positive outcome may be realized if this radical change takes place.

Consider the fact that it is very easy to make the past a source of unhappiness. If only life had treated me differently! If only I had not been inflicted by nature, fate, poor health, parents, relatives, teachers, bosses, and all those other people who brought me to my present state, I could be happy. So I live in a constant state of what the psychiatrist Albert Ellis calls "awfulizing," and I am engaged in the pursuit of unhappiness. To be a part of our society that, Ellis contends, is to have an abundance of illogical ideas and philosophies that lead to self-defeating patterns or neurosis.[3]

As a marriage and family therapist, I have known many couples whom I thought could make a stable marriage but who unnecessarily destroy it. Numerous divorces occur because the couple has learned over the years how to become utterly miserable, and they practice what they have learned. They are constantly looking at past mistakes and grievances and they will not let go. There is hidden anger over unresolved conflicts. If only people would learn that in many cases in marriage, unfortunate events can happen, conflicts will arise, but they need not be serious. Forgive, learn from mistakes, and move ahead with a commitment to seek the promises that a married life can bring.

Looking back at the past might be called the "Mrs. Lot syndrome." The story is found in Genesis 19. The angels told Lot and his family to get out of Sodom and Gomorrah as it was about to be destroyed. But they lingered—it is so difficult to leave a Sodom and Gomorrah! So men took them to the edge of the city, gave them a hefty shove, and said, "Flee for your life; do not look back or stop anywhere in the Plain; flee to the hills, or else you will be consumed" (v. 17). But as they ran for the hills, Mrs. Lot looked back and was turned to a "pillar of salt." Why did she turn back? Was she lamenting the past with one long, last look? As a result, she lost both the past and the future.

Use that story as a metaphor and say, flee from the evil past, let it burn and don't look back. For in so doing one might be turned into a salty pillar of remorse and regret. It is impossible to go back to or change the past. The failures, the sins, the mistakes are written and the chapters are finished. To try to modify or distort them is an exercise in futility. But Christians believe in forgiveness—from God and from those we have wronged—*if we ask for it*. From that grace and that forgiveness, we can go on into a new life.

The decisions that we make are rarely perfect. But if we make a decision based on our best judgment and with God's help, we should let it stand. Sandra Day O'Connor, Supreme Court Justice, said in a talk she made in 1996, "When I'm at the court faced with a case, I try to find out everything about that case I can. Then I make my decision, and I don't look back. I do not look back and say, 'Oh, what if I had done the other thing,' or 'Oh, I should have done something else.'"

Not only must we learn to deal with the past, but what about our hopes for the future? In our culture we are taught to be achievers and in some cases, perfectionists—from Little League to big business. This seems to be a worthy goal for most of us, but we can allow it to make us miserable. No one of us ever reaches his or her potential—only a small percentage of it. We can always be better than we are. Improvement is always possible. To become perfect, the situation is hopeless but not serious.

I have a picture in which I am shaking hands with Arnold Palmer. It was taken long ago. Arnold had just finished a round of golf in an exhibition match held in my hometown. I followed him all around the course. Then I said to myself, someday I want to play like Arnold Palmer. For over thirty years I have been trying to reach that goal. The situation is hopeless but not serious. I can still enjoy a game of golf as a high handicapper. When I saw Greg Norman miss a twelve-inch putt in the U.S. Open, I said, "I can do that, too." Why should either he or I be unhappy about it? These things happen.

I have had the privilege of shaking hands with a few famous people. I shook hands with Jimmy Durante in Chicago as we descended in an elevator at the Palmer House. I like to use humor, but I will never be as funny as he was. I had a chance to talk with Walter Cronkite before he spoke at a convention in Scottsdale, Arizona. I read widely, but I will never be as erudite as he is. I rode in a parlor car from Chicago to Champaign, Illinois, seated next to Duke Ellington. I like to play the piano, but I will never play like Duke Ellington. The situation is hopeless but not serious. It is not serious because I am not talented in their skills, but I can be a real person in my own right. I will never preach like Peter nor pray like Paul, but I can minister in my own way and be acceptable to God in that role. You and I are not perfect, but we are unique—there is no one like us in the whole world. After God created each of us, he destroyed the mold. Never forget—we are not perfect but that is not serious—because we *are* extraordinary.

You may be in a state right now that is better than that which you think yourself to be—and not know it! Count your blessings! Thank God for what you have. Open your eyes and your heart. We are the recipients of bountiful gifts from a giving God.

Again consider there are no perfect and final answers to some of the disturbing questions that we face. Some problems will never be solved, although we should keep on trying to solve them. Some areas will always remain a mystery in spite of our efforts to explain them.

I don't comprehend the ways of the universe in all its vastness. I don't understand how a flower grows or understand the impervious movements of the hummingbird that sips nectar from the feeder on our patio. I can't explain how I get out of bed each morning and walk from one place to another. Many aspects of life are enigmas to me. Yet I enjoy the mystery of all of it. A fruit-grower said to me, "I don't know how a tree produces apples, but I enjoy eating the apples." I relish life in spite of a thousand unanswered questions.

Larry King has said on his programs that he wasn't religious because no one had ever given him a satisfactory answer to the question, "Who made God?" Of course not. To answer that would be equivalent to trying to explain to a Siamese cat who designed the Golden Buddha in a temple in Bangkok. The situation is hopeless but not serious. I can't answer that question, but I know that God exists. Through the years God has entered my life in many ways. In Jesus Christ I know that God is and what he is like. There are divine mysteries beyond my ability to comprehend. This makes life all the more intriguing and it keeps me humble.

Do we believe that there will come a time when we will be absolutely and completely happy *all of the time*? Is that our life goal? A bit of ancient wisdom tells us, there will be times when we are sad, discouraged, stressed out, depressed. This is at one end of the swing of the pendulum of life as it moves from agony to ecstasy and back. This is a part of everyone's life. God did not promise that we would live forever in a rose garden. There may be times when the situation may seem hopeless, but how serious is it, if we have faith in a God who cares?

Why do people put so much effort in seeking happiness as their life goal? I think I know. We have been carefully taught, systematically conditioned, preached to from the press, the radio, and television that we can have things that will make us happy. We have come to believe that through these things, our search for happiness will be rewarded eventually by our becoming happy. But what is being "happy"? And why does it so often fly away like a frightened bird when we try to catch it? I have often thought about this when a young couple comes to me for premarital counseling. I always ask them, "Why do you want to be married?" The answer is almost always the same: "Because we are in love!" I am tempted to reply, "And are you *in* anything else?" I believe in love in the best sense of that word. Why is it that so many couples "in love" marry, expecting to be happy, and fail to attain happiness? In many cases their expectations of what marriage can do for them are vastly exaggerated. To expect perfection in marriage is a hopeless dream. All married couples have a variety of problems, but these difficulties need not seriously damage the relationship if proper skills and attitudes are maintained.

Many couples don't find fulfillment in life because they are looking for the right answers in the wrong places: a large salary, a luxurious home, success in business, plus a relationship undisturbed by problems and conflicts. Married life involves something more than they anticipated before they were married. A former student of mine wrote after she had been married a year, "Why didn't you tell me what marriage is really like?" I thought I had. Why had her dreams faded? If we would stand back and view the situation, we would see how hopeless it is to look for something when it isn't there.

Paul Watzlawick proposes the following situation. "Under a street lamp there stands a man, slightly intoxicated, who is searching for something. In the lighted area he searches over and over. A policeman comes along, asks him what he is looking for, and the man answers, 'My keys.' Now they both search. After a while the policeman wants to know whether the man is sure that he lost his keys here, and the latter answers, 'No, not here, back there—but there it is much too dark.'"[4] Absurd? Yet that is what many do. They are looking where it is convenient or pleasurable to look, not where they should look. That is hopeless—but not serious if they would turn around and look in the place where that which is lost can be found.

This tragedy is repeated over and over. For this reason, the proposed solution to the situation *becomes the problem*. When what we believe to be the answer becomes the problem, we are in trouble. A parent screams at a child. The child continues to disobey. The parent screams louder. The child continues to disobey. The parent becomes violent and strikes the child. The parent's solution to the child's behavior *becomes the problem*. This *is* serious because it is a state where trying harder simply intensifies the problem.

How tragic is the life of people who search for happiness and satisfaction in the wrong places. What they seek to make them happy becomes their problem.

When we move from the personal to the larger social scene, we face some of the same problems. We all want peace. Where are we looking for solutions? We spend at least $250 billion a year on a worldwide military empire. That is approximately $3,730 per family. Should it cost that much to maintain a secure defense system? Are we looking for our true defenses in the wrong places? What could really make our nation strong? Better education and health care should have more attention. We need to clean the pollution from our lakes and rivers. Global warming threatens our future. We all want to reduce our national debt. Billions are squandered in waste, fraud, and pork-barrel appropriations! Are we looking in the right places? We must seek solutions in the right places that will truly safeguard our future.

Reinhold Niebuhr wrote,

> In the realm of economics . . . an efficient economy was the product of a secularism, which began by regarding happiness as the final end of life, continued by substituting comfort and security for happiness and ended by regarding

efficiency as an end in itself." He continued, "The idolatry which substituted a means to an end as the final end of existence has tended to vulgarize our culture. . . . Our gadget-filled culture suspended in a hell of international insecurity certainly does not offer us even the happiness of which the former century dreamed. Only when we realize the cause of these disappointed hopes can we have a truly religious culture."[5]

We must not be deceived by the illusions of a secular age. We need to look humbly and realistically at the right places to find the causes that have brought us to where we are in our vulgarized culture. Then we can act to bring health and a sound future for our civilization.

We all want something that will give us satisfaction and security. Where are we looking in order to find what we really need—in friendly, well-lit places—the casinos of life—in prosperity theology—in more arms and ammunition? Solutions are often in darker, more obscure areas, where it takes courage, honesty, intelligence, and ingenuity to search and find!

I stated at the beginning that the solution is relatively clear—it is as lucid as the Gospel itself. Read the Sermon on the Mount, particularly that portion in chapter 6 of Matthew. Jesus is looking at all the people who are trying to achieve their life goals by being anxious about the accumulation of things. Stephen Carter in the Utne Reader ponders the conundrum of why Americans, with the highest standard of living in the world, are so unhappy. He says it is partly because they do not know that some things are more important than others. Exactly!

Therefore, do not worry or make yourselves miserable by troubling yourselves over what you are going to eat, or what kind of clothes you must have. For it is those of little faith who spend most of their time with concerns for these things. God knows you have to have food and clothing, but are they the most important? So put your first priority in the plan God has for you in his kingdom rule, with all its values and goodness. And in so doing you also will have all of the things you need. Do not be anxious about tomorrow. Just take care of today. (Matt. 6:25–34, au. trans.)

I don't believe Jesus promised his disciples what is ordinarily termed "happiness." In many places he seems to imply something quite different. "Blessed are those who are persecuted for righteousness' sake, for theirs is the kingdom of heaven" (Matt. 5:10). Seeking the kingdom of heaven might prove to be quite costly. "Then Jesus told his disciples, 'If any want to become my followers, let them deny themselves and take up their cross and follow me. . . . For what will it profit them if they gain the whole world but forfeit their life?'" (Mattt. 16:24, 26). What might bearing the cross mean?

If we do bear crosses, there are promises that we can live without worry and fear, for "There is no fear in love, but perfect love casts out fear" (1 John 4:18). And joy: "I have said these things to you so that my joy may be in you, and that your joy may be complete" (John 15:11). Hardship, illness, misfortune cannot be avoided, but they can be overcome and transformed.

Sometimes in grief and sadness, there is a "rainbow through the rain" kind of joy. It is in the love of Christ and in the love of neighbor that we find what we really need—a fulfilled life—the "abundant life." It is here life can be lived with courage, joy, meaning, and love. Is it too simple to believe that one's supply of love can never run out, for in the giving, the supply is renewed! In *agape* there is a deep cup that runneth over. We drink and are filled.

For each of us there is an end to this earthly life. It is this love of Christ that takes away the "sting of death"! Paul speaks about this in 1 Corinthians 15. Some years ago, the Presbyterian Church asked Stan Freeburg, the humorist and satirist, to write a few radio scripts to depict some of the spiritual truths that might be helpful to the general public. In one segment, two men talk, and as they prepare to depart, one asks the other, "Do you have a card?" The man gives him his card. "But this card is in pencil!" "Yes," replies the other, "we are all just penciled in." So we are! To live permanently on this earth is hopeless but not serious. In life and death we are in the hands of a loving God.

What about the "sting" of living in the present? We pick up the morning paper. Bad news! We turn on the television—another homicide, one more child abused, a spouse beaten and perhaps killed, a terrorist bombing, a plane crash! There are wars and dissension in so many parts of the world. There is fraud and deceit in high places and in low places, far away and near to home. There are hungry people in the world. Millions are homeless. As Christians, how are we to respond?

I find myself vacillating between optimism and pessimism, between elation and sadness. I am sure others do as well. Many people are more depressed than hopeful. This current stage of depression has been called the "common cold of the psyche." How can we transform this depressive state into a zest for life? Let me speak for myself.

I must remember there are many things I cannot change. Yet, through it all, I will live by faith—faith in a God who sent his Son into the world to redeem the world. I stand with him in that redemption through bad times and good. I will seek the kingdom the best I can. I will not invite misery to come into my life over matters I cannot alter. I will change what I can. I will try to find the good life in places where it can be found and not where it does not exist.

"So if anyone is in Christ, there is a new creation: everything old has passed away; see, everything has become new! All this is from God, who reconciled us to himself through Christ, and has given us the ministry of reconciliation" (2 Cor. 5:17–18). Happiness no longer becomes a restless, relentless, futile search for something that is not there.

Through that which is deemed hopeless—the present—there arises a fresh hope, a new vision, and a world of creative possibilities.

It is in the dead of night. Sodom and Gomorrah, the evil city, is burning behind us. In that burning are all the tragedies of yesterday—the pretensions, the stupidities, the ambiguities, and the moral breakdowns. We have learned hard lessons, but we will not look back. Putting our hands in the hand of God, we will move toward the hills and the dawning of a new day.

Acrimony and Grace

Vic Jameson

*O*ur acquaintance began in acrimony, and there was plenty of basis for supposing it would remain that way. The fact that it changed—the *reason* it changed—makes the story worth telling.

Some of the ill feeling was mine. A hostile article had been published about the magazine. I had responded in print. Some readers had written agreeing with what I said; others—more of them—disagreed. People on both sides had strong opinions and expressed them.

You may have noticed an absence of detail here on the subject of the dispute. That's intentional; the story to be told is about something that happened as a result of the dispute, and does not need to be cluttered by the pros and cons of the argument.

So back to the story:

One of the letters received in response to my column was a masterpiece of denouncement. With thorough and stinging precision it sliced up everything I'd said. It covered two and a half single-spaced typewritten pages and it didn't waste a word.

Not every letter to the editor gets a personal answer, or requires one. On this subject, though, I had decided all of them should be acknowledged.

So when the two-and-half-page classic had been read and reread, I settled down to answer it. What emerged was a rebuttal equally long, equally detailed, and, I'm afraid, equally vigorous. I finished it late in the day and decided to let it cool overnight.

Sometimes you do things without exactly knowing why. For whatever reason, the next morning I reread my embattled reply and threw it away. I couldn't have given you a reason, but I felt better for having done it. Then I wrote a three-sentence response to the letter and mailed it. It wasn't a soft answer. It described the man's letter with the word "vituperative," and it mentioned our plans to publish it in full.

It was when the telephone rang three or four days later that the unexpected began.

A call demanding that we not publish the letter wouldn't have been surprising. But it wasn't to say that at all.

"Your letter set me thinking," he said, and added that recent times "have been a low point in my life." There had been a serious and costly financial problem where he worked. Death had taken away some people dear to him and stamped its mark on others. There was more that clearly had been painful both professionaly and personally. "And I guess I just snapped," he said, "and took it all out on you."

He continued, "Those things that happened are no excuse for doing what I did, and I don't use them as excuses. I've called you to apologize."

Apology accepted, of course, I said, and fumbled for the right words to say to someone much more gracious and gutsy than I. Then he added:

"I have a Communion service to go to today. I've written you a letter, but I had to talk to you and ask your forgiveness before I go to Communion."

I said "Of course" again, still not finding adequate, appropiate words to add. We had never seen each other, but we had been, if not bitter enemies, at least antagonists hurling harsh words at each other through the mail. Now, abruptly, we were asking and pledging prayers by and for each other. Pledges that are being kept.

Writers are supposed to know how to explain things like that, but I don't. Not yet, anyway. I believe something immensely significant happened, but I can neither explain it nor fathom exactly how it came to be.

But I know that, for me, because of that telephone conversation, World Communion Sunday is going to have an extra dimension of meaning this year.

Grandfather's Prayers

J. Marshall Jenkins

*L*ast year, I visited my grandfather, C. Rees Jenkins, at the infirmary of Sharon Towers, a Presbyterian retirement home in Charlotte, North Carolina. I arrived just as my aunt was reading Scripture very loudly into his hearing aid. I waited outside.

Grandfather was ninety-four years old at the time, a retired Presbyterian minister who had served as a missionary in Japan before World War II, pastor to several churches, chaplain in a Veterans Administration (VA) hospital, and leader of a prison ministry in Charlotte. He retired during my childhood, but until recently I knew him as a blur of perpetual motion. There were souls to save, words of good news to proclaim, broken spirits to minister unto in the name of Christ. He did not much care whether the biblical interpretation was fundamentalist or liberal, whether the pastoral care was authoritarian or submissive, whether he ministered to a prisoner or a CEO. He had no time to quibble over details until Christ blew the whistle and announced the job was done.

His blur of activity had ended two years before when his wife died. Now when anyone asks him how he is doing, he makes it quite clear that he sees no point in waiting another day for God to call him to rejoin her. But after a lifetime of obedience, he will not press the issue. She was his eyes, ears, and memory, so he is confused, cannot find his other sock, and cannot remember names. But he still has his legs. When he meanders into the hallway each morning, smells the antiseptic smell, and sees the clinical corridor, he is a VA chaplain again. He pays a pastoral visit to each of his fellow geriatric patients, sometimes four or five times in the same morning.

"Amen," I heard my aunt and my grandfather say together, and her chair slid a bit as she got up to leave. He said something to her that I could not make out, but everyone on the hall could hear her shouted reply, "All we need is for you to keep praying! Just keep praying. Nothing is more important than that!" I have shouted the same thing at him many times, and I know the question well. By the end of every visit, this man of God asks for some clue that no mortal can give, some answer to the question: Is my life worth living in this interim between my wife's death and mine? Is there anything I can do to get past this loneliness, this sense of worthlessness? Anything I can do for you, for the barely alive man in room 210, for the nurse, for the Lord?

No, Granddad, there is nothing you can do. Or said another way, there is everything you can do. All we need is for you to keep praying. Just keep praying. Nothing is more important than that. When he moved to this small infirmary to live out the rest of his days with constant nursing care, we shipped out the remainder of his large library of theological books. But he kept several dog-eared, yellowing books filled with names of missionaries, Bible translators, friends, and family members. Among them, my name. Each day, for hour upon lonely hour, he leafs through these lists of names and prays for them—for missionaries he never met and for his own children and grandchildren.

All we need, Granddad, is for you to keep praying. Just keep praying. Nothing is more important than that. Admittedly, when his children and grandchildren say that, our hurried, distracted, unbelieving spirits say, Don't bother me with a question I cannot answer. Don't ask me what you can do in this interim between death and life to make yourself worthy of God's love. I don't even know how to make myself worthy of God's love. If you don't know after ninety-four years of sainted ministry, I don't know.

All we need, Granddad, is for you to keep praying. If we say it to him enough, maybe we will believe it. Nothing is more important. Not running this nursing home. Not running this big southern city. Not even, in the end, running from room to room paying pastoral visits and spreading the good news.

My aunt departed. Granddad and I greeted each other warmly, and the conversation began. "Now where is it you live again, boy?" he asked, apologizing three times for forgetting, then apologizing three more times after I answered.

"Now you are . . . your name is . . ." I told him, and he apologized again. I managed to make a joke of it and we laughed.

"Now what do you do again?" I told him. "Oh yes, a fine work, a fine work indeed. I wish you lived in Charlotte, but if the Lord wants you down there. . . . Where is it you live again?"

And around we went for a while until I pulled out some essays I had written and read them to him. I knew he could not make out what I said. But I wrote them and I was reading them, so he wanted to hear them. I read to him passages from the Bible, and he heard the words, I could tell, because he echoed them softly and rocked along with them as if hearing a favorite song on the radio.

Finally, we prayed together. We prayed for each other in our own various ways that say we love each other, ways that affirm God's love for the other even if, here between death and life, we each felt perplexed about our own worthiness. And for a moment, it occurred to me that I was the beneficiary of countless more prayers prayed in this place. It occurred to me that God may be less lonely in this place filled with prayers than in most of creation.

God created us "so that [we] would search for God and perhaps grope for him and find him—though indeed he is not far from each one of us" (Acts 17:27). Not far from my grandfather in the deafness and confusion of his infirmary. Not far from his children and grandchildren in our bewilderment over the meaning of his life and our own. Not far from those on or off his prayer list who forget to pray but who search and grope more desperately for an unknown God. In the end, all we need is for those in places filled with prayers to keep praying until time or calling brings us to inhabit those places, to search, and find. And be found. Nothing is more important.

Saints and Writers: On Doing One's Work in Hiding

Belden C. Lane

I have stopped for coffee in the Central West End, putting off the writing that awaits me in my office. Starting is hard, in writing as it is in life. Most of us would rather be known for having written than endure the agony of writing. We would rather have a reputation for saintliness than live a saintly life. Why is it that striving for the appearance of good work is always easier than doing it?

What I offer here is a reflection on the craft of writing and its relation to the lives of the saints. It wrestles with some of the difficulties Stephanie Paulsell identifies in her recent essay on "Writing as a Spiritual Discipline."[1] She describes Marguerite d'Oingt, a French Carthusian nun, working in the scriptorium of her thirteenth-century monastery, trying to express in words she does not yet possess the mystery and ambiguity of her own spiritual life. It's a dilemma shared by every writer who takes up the pen in the effort to live her way more fully into faith. The questions I raise relate particularly to the authorial self and the problems that writers in the field of spirituality confront in asserting, and also disclaiming, their narrative voice. How does one write for others about holy things without falling into the trap of taking oneself too seriously?

There is a crippling self-consciousness that accompanies the embrace of any spiritual discipline. It comes from paying too much attention to the people we imagine are watching. Anxious writers fantasize about the legions of readers awaiting—with earnest judgment or delight—every word they put to paper. Only in getting older do we realize that most people had never been watching (or reading) us at all. We could have had a field day, throwing ourselves into reckless freedom, had we known it all along. Saints and writers recognize the danger of yielding too much to the fear of criticism or a longing for praise. The difference is that the saints act on it, while writers usually do not. The saints remind us that whatever we do well in our lives we do without thought of an audience.

Some things I can't write as freely as I'd like, for example, with the academy looking over my shoulder. So I stop here on Friday mornings, at a safe distance from the university, escaping the critical glance of deans and journal editors and peer-review committees. I chain up my bike at the St. Louis Bread Company, sit at a table by the window, and scribble in the journal as a way of reentering the work. It is like pouring a can of rainwater down the spout of a rusty pump, then furiously working the handle until the prime catches and the water flows. Once in a while it works.

Practicing Self-Forgetfulness

I know that writing itself should not be so difficult. It is not a matter of imagining oneself as Lord Byron on a mountain top, said Brenda Ueland. It is more like "a child stringing beads in kindergarten—happy, absorbed and quietly putting one bead on after another."[2] But doing it with the child's *self-forgetfulness—that* is the tricky part. That alone is what lends purity and simplicity to the work. The anonymous fourteenth-century author of *The Book of Privy Counseling* spoke of the perfect lover (if not the perfect writer) as "enwrapped in a full and final forgetting of himself."[3] Embracing this arduous task of self-abandonment is the hardest part of writing. But it is the only thing that qualifies it as a spiritual exercise.

Popular images of saints and writers overemphasize their singularity of vision, their bold intentionality and self-clarity—the things that most evoke public admiration. But in finishing their work, the truth is that the best of them usually had no idea of the worth of what they had done. Its significance was concealed from them altogether. Most saints and writers are at best inadvertent heroes, the only ones with whom we readily identify. Like Frodo and Sam in Tolkien's *Lord of the Rings*, they succeed—if at all—because of their anonymity, their bumbling simplicity and determined faithfulness to a quest that others thought absurd.

The hugely "successful" writers and saints are, indeed, the ones who most deserve our sympathy. Being acclaimed for either wit or sanctity is usually more curse than blessing. It breeds a corrupting self-awareness that cloys mind and heart alike. Only an ascetic renunciation (sometimes seclusion or wild eccentricity or another form of the *via negativa*) can keep the soul from turning in on itself. In the Roman Catholic canonization process, the more dead one is, the better his or her chance of even being considered for sainthood. The recognition of sanctity is principally a postmortem operation. Notoriety in one's lifetime guarantees nothing. It is not even a gift.

John Updike wrote in his memoirs, to which he gave the title *Self-Consciousness*, that "celebrity is a mask that eats into the face. As soon as one is aware of being 'somebody,' to be watched and listened to with extra interest, input ceases, and the performer goes blind and deaf in his overanimation. One can either see or be seen. Most of the best fiction is written out of early impressions, taken in before the writer became conscious of himself as a writer."[4]

The same is undoubtedly true of saints. John Climacus, like the other Desert Christians, continually emphasized *apatheia* (or holy indifference) as contributing more than anything else to the practice of holy living. To have one's productivity undercelebrated, if not even ignored, by one's contemporaries is actually a gift, he insisted.[5] It certainly isn't an indication of not being loved. It may, in fact, be the only way of knowing love. Holy indifference demands a clear separation of one's work from one's worth as a person. This protects the integrity of the work, on the one hand, while assuring the worker that love is never a consequence of productivity, on the other. Natalie Goldberg cautions in her book *Writing Down the Bones* that one should not use writing to get love.[6] Compulsively seeking the reader's approval destroys the whole process. Reassurance has to come from elsewhere.

Oddly enough, James Joyce received his greatest encouragement as a writer from his wife Nora, a woman who paid little attention to anything he ever wrote. Brenda Maddox, her biographer, says of Joyce, "Nora's indifference to his work saddened and tantalized him. It was part of her desirability and unattainability that his genius was of no interest to her. She loved him for his ordinariness."[7] With the critics, he always had to second-guess himself. With Nora, he never had to prove anything. It was useless even to try. Loving indifference can provide a safe place—a hidden center—from which one's creativity grows without being turned back onto itself.

Starting and Hiding

So I wrestle here with these two dilemmas in the writing life, echoed as they are in the spiritual life as well. How do you get started, overcoming the noonday demon of sloth (*acci-die*)? And how do you distance yourself from the watchful, numbing eyes of real and imagined critics? Starting and hiding, these are the necessary skills to which saints and writers ever return. How do they repeatedly enter the simplicity of new beginnings and how do they escape the paralyzing effects of self-consciousness? Being able to hide may often be the key to knowing how to start.

An undisclosed center—an interior point at which one remains utterly blind to outside evaluation, whether praise or blame—lies necessarily at the core of saintly writing and saintly living. The anxious ego has no claim here, no need to conform to the expectations of others. If our work does not come from such a place, we will never experience freedom in what we do. We will remain outside our truest selves, disconnected, living forever in the thought-world of others.

Seeking one's own center, however, does not mean discounting the importance of criticism. Spiritual direction is as crucial to the life of the spirit as good editing is to the life of the mind. Both deliver us from the blindness of the solitary thinker, the parochialness of the isolated believer. Thomas Wolfe would never have been disciplined as a writer without the help of Maxwell Perkins, his editor at Scribners. Thomas Merton depended heavily on the honest feedback of his agent, Naomi Burton. Jane de Chantal attributed her success in the spiritual life to her friend and mentor, Francis de Sales. Irish saints relied on the often harsh but sensitive leadership of the *anamchara* (soul friend).

Yet the director's best work, the editor's finest achievement, is in pointing the disciple (or writer) back to the center of his or her own creativity. Sound criticism allows us to do cleanly and simply what arises most naturally out of the hidden place within. It gives us back to ourselves, stripped of ostentation and cant.[8]

Formed, then, by the critical disciplines that writing demands—indeed, profoundly grateful for them—I stop from time to time at the Bread Company to write from the inner place that criticism has helped to clarify and protect. I put the university at arm's length, entertaining for a moment the mystery of "hiding" and "starting" that life is always demanding of us. People pass by on the sidewalk. Birds gather under the sweet-gum tree outside. I fill up the pages of a long yellow pad—writing whatever comes, working in the quiet disregard of contentment. I censor nothing. Nor does anyone pay attention to this balding man sitting in the corner alone.

I am aware, like Yeats, that "my fiftieth year has come and gone, / I sit, a solitary man, / in a crowded London shop / an open book and empty cup / on the marble table-top." When I am lucky on such a day, when "for twenty minutes more or less / it seems, so great my happiness," the words begin to flow. The body blazes and I know myself blessed, and able to bless.[9] Light comes pouring through the window, and I am a child stringing beads again.

Unfortunately, every time I come back to the "sublime writing" of that ecstatic moment, it is never as brilliant as I remembered. Often it is fluff. But I delight nonetheless in the memory of that short-lived experience of freedom in writing. It is like the irrepressibility of glossalalia in speech, more beautiful than any of the ideas that surface within it. In this brief interval, internalized critical voices are silenced. Control is abandoned. For a blessed few moments, I write in unchecked, unself-conscious immediacy.

What *is* this experience? Is it akin to what the Desert Christians taught as the wakeful attentiveness of *agrupnia* (sleeplessness, watching), what Buddhist monk Thich Nhat Hahn teaches as the "miracle of mindfulness"?[10] Is it the experience of "entering a zone" that basketball players and long-distance runners describe when they're caught up in the intensity of the moment, no longer aware of themselves? Actors and musicians now and then experience the same thing in a performance. Social psychologist Mihaly Csiks-zentmihalyi says that in an experience of "flow," one action follows another without need for conscious intervention.[11] We move in concert with everything around us. Intentionality yields to spontaneity. The spirit breathes us.

The ordinary process of writing (or holy living, for that matter) rarely approximates anything of this sort. It is dull as nails most of the time, and rightly so. Even John Coltrane never again discovered that perfect and unplayable note that had come to him late one night in a jazz riff, carrying him where he had never been before. Yet these rare experiences of "flow" remind us how much we depend for the purity of our work on the disappearance of the calculating self. That is what we seek, even if we seldom realize it. In rare moments, it is what allows a writer (or a saint) to stand in amazement at what has been written (or lived)—seeing one's work as coming, it would seem, from wholly outside oneself.

Invisible Saints and the Writer's Anonymity

There is a yet deeper dimension of hiddenness in the isolated experience of certain writers and saints. More impressive than passing experiences of "flow" and egoless creativity, is the still rarer gift of being able do one's work without *ever* discerning its full significance. To keep stringing beads like a child, happily and absorbingly—to accept the enduring uncertainty of the worth of one's work through the whole of one's life—is to enter the most difficult (and powerful) hiddenness we know. We find it, for example, in obscure desert fathers like Romanus and Chomas, about whom we know virtually nothing—in each case only a single sentence remembered from the last words spoken on their deathbed.[12] A whole life condensed into little more than a dozen words. Even more telling is the ability of some writers to trust in the unrelieved darkness of rejection, people like Emily Dickinson and Gerard Manley Hopkins who doggedly stayed at their work, remaining virtually unpublished as long as they lived. What sustains both writers and saints in the depths of such obscurity?

Accounts of hidden saints recur in all the religious and folk traditions of the world. These are holy individuals never publicly recognized for their sanctity, usually unknown even to themselves. Canonization (or recognition of any sort) would compromise the integrity of their work. Their "ministry" depends largely on their incognito. In the Jewish tradition, for example, these are the *Lamed-Vovnik*—the thirty-six righteous individuals who at any given moment uphold the earth by the hidden power of their lives. Because of their faithfulness, God promises to sustain all that lives. If only one of these were lacking, says André Schwarz-Bart, humanity would suffocate with a single cry.[13]

In Islamic mysticism, the *kutb* (literally "pole" or "axis," the pivot around which everything else revolves) is the most perfect human being living at any given time. Opinions vary as to the whereabouts of the *kutb*, but many insist that he (or she) necessarily remains undivulged, exercising the centeredness of the world from deep within hiding.[14] In Buddhist thought, the Bodhisattvas are compassionate beings who have postponed their entrance into Nirvana in order to be available to those in need. They often descend in the guise of ministering angels to perform hidden deeds of mercy.

We inadvertently share in the unknown lives of these saints when in solitude we attend to our work with the same carefulness as we do when others are watching. Rilke insisted in his *Letters to a Young Poet* that one's motivation in writing can never come from outside. It has to emerge as a necessity of the soul, an inner command one must obey regardless of what others may think.[15] To remain determinedly at one's work— knowing that writing (or praying) is simply what one *has* to do. To choose happily to work, knowing full well that there is no other choice. That is the joy at the heart of creativity. On the days when writing is hard it means simply keeping the fingers moving, like Jews dovening at prayer, as if the wiggling of the pen on paper (or the movement of fingers on keys) were itself somehow honoring to God—wholly apart from the results that come. One writes, in such moments, as one must pray. The exercise becomes an end in itself, pursued without thought of consequence.

Secrecy in the Spiritual Life

To write from the quiet resolve and secretiveness of this center is particularly important for those who do spiritual writing—who necessarily live their way into the truth they describe, using their own experience to draw their readers into its fullness. The saints are the ones who do it best. Their effort is not simply to communicate an idea, but to transgenerate an experience. Doing this in their writing often requires a high degree of self-disclosure. Their problem is knowing how to model in some frail way the shape their truth can take in the lives of their readers without calling undue attention to themselves. Learning how to get out of the way is the most difficult task in spiritual writing.[16]

The most widely read spiritual writers of the last generation—from Thomas Merton and Henri Nouwen to Frederick Buechner and Kathleen Norris—wrestled with this dilemma. How do you write about spirituality in the first person while still remaining hidden? How do you reveal yourself, touching what is most universal and deeply human in the reader, while also concealing what belongs only to God or what simply distracts by focusing on the author's peculiar idiosyncrasies? This raises the theological question of the incarnation itself. Even God, said Karl Barth, cannot unveil himself to us in any other way than by veiling himself.[17] Genuine disclosure necessitates a practice of hiding.

Merton, as a Trappist monk, openly wrote of his continuing difficulties with Abbot James at Gethsemani, even of falling in love with a nurse in Louisville, Kentucky. Nouwen wrestled publicly with all of his demons, trying to write his way into a freedom he never quite realized. Buechner spoke of the unspeakable in disclosing his father's suicide. Norris has written guardedly of her husband's mental illness.[18] Each author has struggled with knowing how much to say, and what *not* to say, in modeling a spirituality to which they invite their readers' entrance. They walk a narrow edge, trying not to step outside the hiddenness that necessarily protects them and their readers.

They know that if you do not guard this privacy with a fierce resolve, if your audience is drawn into all your secrets, if you are willing to say anything for the sake of public adulation, you lose your soul as well as the quality of your work. A false intimacy destroys what it pretends to foster. No matter how much is told in the writer's self-disclosure or the saint's openness of soul, what is *not* told in the secrecy of one's presence before God becomes the power that animates the rest of one's speech.

This is a perennial danger in the cult of the saints. We want to know everything about our public heroes, reaching for the hidden details of their lives while turning them into marketable stereotypes of this or that imagined virtue. Merton, for example, has been at the top of the charts for years, both as writer and as saint. There is a Merton for every marketing niche— Merton as beat poet, war resistor, monastic rebel, contemplative master, compulsive writer, Eastern guru wannabe. He has become as much a victim of his own self-disclosure as of his readers' desire to romanticize his life. His propensity to self-divulgence was extraordinary (even obsessive), especially for someone trying to recover for the twentieth century the gifts of the apophatic tradition. While he knew in his heart that "what is best is what is not said," it took him thousands of pages to empty himself of everything but the unsaying.[19] Knowing how to preserve mystery and secrecy in the spiritual life is as indispensable to those who write about it as to those who live it.

Strategies of Hiddenness

That is why saintly writers through the history of Christian spirituality have employed various strategies of hiddenness in "getting out of the way" of their work. They have exercised the weapon of "holy indifference" both inwardly and outwardly, with respect to their own authorial voice and with regard to their readers. They have practiced "being dead, their lives hid with Christ in God," as George Herbert put it anagrammatically in his poem "Colossians 3:3."[20]

Some of the best spiritual writers have been wholly anonymous, like the fourteenth-century English author of *The Cloud of Unknowing*. Others have taken the approach of "Dionysius the Areopagite," an undisclosed sixth-century monk from Syria who penned his remarkable mystical writings under the pseudonym of the apostle Paul's companion in first-century Athens. Dag Hammarskjöld never mentioned to others the "markings" he had been writing all through his life. They were discovered on a bedside table at his death, surprising the world by the unknown depths of the career diplomat's inner life. Teachers of emptiness have known intrinsically that they teach best by the negation of their own self-consciousness.

Søren Kierkegaard made frequent use of pseudonymous authorship, sometimes to disguise himself from the Danish public for whom he wrote, at other times to disclose parts of himself to Regina Olsen, the woman he loved. Other authors have exercised varying degrees of self-effacement in their writing, detracting from their own authority or credibility in numerous ways. Julian of Norwich diminished her importance in her *Showings of Divine Love*, minimizing her role in receiving God's truth—not simply to disarm her critics (especially those suspicious of women having visions), but also to emphasize the universal applicability of the truth she was given.[21] Barth employed self-deprecating humor in discounting the lengthy volumes of his *Church Dogmatics*. He wrote of the angels laughing at old Karl, trying to enter heaven with his pushcart full of books.[22] These are efforts at disarming the attention of others so as to focus on what matters most—the author's quiet and faithful commitment to the work he has been given.

Certainly it is time I did that myself, heading on to the office now to attend to the writing I have been avoiding all this while by sitting here writing about writing. People who write will do anything to delay the necessity of their work. Starting is that difficult. Distractions are endless. You will sit down at the computer to work and suddenly the need to dust the molding over the door to your office will present itself as a matter of enormous importance, something you have irresponsibly neglected for years. In the moment of starting, *anything* is more fascinating than writing. That is why a discipline, even a ritual activity, may be crucial to the process of hiding that starting requires.

Writers do crazy things to get out of themselves, to facilitate the discipline of their attentiveness. Hemingway obsessively sharpened his pencils and wrote standing up. Schiller kept the smell of rotten apples under the lid of his desk. Alexandre Dumas wrote his nonfiction on rose-colored paper, his fiction on blue, and his poetry on yellow.[23] One does what one has to do. And it is different for everyone.

I will go back to the office now, for example, where I will sit at the desk and light a candle. That is what I do when I mean business. I will pick up my copy, leaning against the computer, of Andre Rublev's fourteenth-century icon of the Holy Trinity. An ivory tower stands in its upper left-hand corner. That is where I work—the university. Contemplating the icon, I will take myself out of the tower, tracing a path down to the bottom of the scene, at the base of a table around which the three persons of the Trinity are seated. Like a child playing in kindergarten, I will imagine myself sneaking up to the small drawer in the side of that table, crawling into it and pulling it shut behind me. The members of the Trinity will pretend not to notice, going along with the game. They will ignore me, as I lie there in the darkness, surrounded by Father, Son, and Holy Spirit speaking together in lively conversation. In that place I will try to write out of the sublime forgetfulness of what I hear.

It's a silly exercise, perhaps. But it's a reminder, that in everything I write, the work is finally not about *me*. It is a way of hiding, of being set free to labor with a measure of joyful unself-consciousness. That is what writers learn best from the saints. It is what allows writing to become an end in itself.

To be published, after all, is not the goal of writing, no more than getting answers is the goal of praying. "Publication," as Anne Lamott writes in her book *Bird by Bird*, "is not all that it is cracked up to be. But writing is. Writing has so much to give, so much to teach, so many surprises. That thing you had to force yourself to do—the actual act of writing—turns out to be the best part."[24] She is right, of course. The hidden work itself, agonizing as it can be, is always the best part.

Everlasting II

Aminta Marks

On an island,
An island washed each day
In the river's rolling, tumbling waves,
You know
Not to fence too many open acres
For the cows to wander off in
When grass is everywhere
And the creeks aren't frozen.

Fence small, green pastures,
Remembering
Winter comes surely.
One year an obstreperous calf wandered off,
Crossed lavish acres and acres of whitening fields,
Got stuck in a snow drift . . . and covered over.
"We couldn't catch those cows . . . they'd run and scatter
Every time we got close," Jeremy remembered.

"To get the cows in before they freeze," he said,
Make sure the water trough
Is where, all summer long,
You've drawn the winter's hay to . . . best
Near an apple tree. They'll always come to ripe apples!"

We listened to an island's lore
All a lazy afternoon
As Jeremy
Who's grown into Buck's everlasting seat on the tractor,
Who's modulated to the family's flow and ebb,
Who was cradled in everlasting waves of hay . . .

Mowing them . . . with Buck . . .

We listened
As Jeremy talked . . .

Described to us the river way.
In this way sense could be made
Of pasturing a herd,
Of a father's life, a father's death,
Of a father's paying everlasting attention
To each single one of his cows,
Utterly nontranscendent, earth strict attention.

The Rondanini Pieta

Aminta Marks

Michelangelo, at last,
Knocked off even the Head
The virgin lifted,
Hacked all polish off,
Let light whack its contra dictions.
He chiseled, out of the Woman's bosom,
The buoyant Head of Man,
His legs a-dangle,
No longer needed to bear His weight,
No longer needed to bear Her weight,
Her Head a flux of His.
Two loves . . . Love
Lifting into the Father.
Jutting angles relaxed,
Embrace becomes a yoke,
We, a light load.
Their spiring
    earthen
        Love
Dumbfounds. Becomes.

The Opportunity and the Imperative to "Be the Presence of Christ"

Derek Maul

I have always been impressed by people who live as if they know exactly what they are doing, whose lives wear a kind of audacity of purpose, every aspiration and action emanating from a deeply held core vision of who they understand themselves to be.

As a child I admired those irrepressible knights of Arthurian legend, who left the sanctity and security of the Round Table to pursue their quest for the Holy Grail; I followed the adventures of the children who found themselves fighting for good in C. S. Lewis's land of Narnia; I read books about people who traveled to faraway places and did difficult things.

My teenage heroes were missionaries: Schweitzer, Livingstone, Cary; and athletes like cricket player C. T. Studd and gold medalist Eric Liddell, both of whom gave up international fame to take the story of Jesus into all the world.

Today, as an adult, I count as mentors folk like Philip Yancy, Richard Foster, Billy Graham, and Mother Teresa—writers and leaders whose integrity of witness has guarded the gospel with dignity in a confused and contentious world.

My wife Rebekah, too, is one of my spiritual heroes, but that is another story.

It is difficult to look at my own life without realizing how badly I have often foundered. I have spent a lot of time hesitating and faltering regarding my purpose and direction, not sure if I was meant to be a teacher, a writer, or maybe something else—as if meaning and purpose could only be found through vocation. I even spent some time at home with our children as a full-time dad. In fact it was there, in my second stint as "house-daddy," that I finally understood God's specific purpose in and through my life, in terms that I could at last understand.

It had been an extremely difficult time for our family, with all the exhaustion and sense of being overwhelmed that parenting frustration can bring. We found ourselves in the middle of such a mixture of grace, trials, blessings, and challenge that I believed we would never see a normal year again—whatever "normal" is supposed to be!

One particularly wearisome day, I was working with our son—the one who God placed in our family to teach us so many things. Once again, the situation represented our ongoing struggle to see clearly and to understand what exactly was going on, especially in the context of the trying year we had just navigated. I remember beginning to angrily express what was on my mind, something critical or hurtful. For once, though, I was able to hold back enough to actually listen to the urgings of the Holy Spirit. It was as if a light suddenly turned on in my heart, and I honestly knew the path that I was meant to take.

"Your job," God told me, "the purpose and the objective that I place now at the center of all that you are, is to *be the presence of Christ* for your son in this situation."

Wow! *Be the presence of Christ*. It was a revolutionary concept to me—challenging, exciting, and a little intimidating—and it still is today when I stop to think about all of the possible implications. But I was able to see the particular trials of that moment in a whole new light. The idea saved me, really, that year, and it has continued to direct my paths and lead me in creative ways ever since.

Be the presence of Christ in my classroom, where I teach severely emotionally disturbed middle-school students. The idea certainly addresses the absurd debate about whether or not God is allowed in the public schools, doesn't it! I may be dealing with a hurting, unreasonable child; a confused and broken parent; or even a cantankerous, intransigent administrator. Whatever the situation, *being the presence of Christ* is an imperative that guides every response, necessarily saturating the environment in prayer from the silence before the first bell to the frenzied end of another day.

Be the presence of Christ in my marriage. Carry with me the opportunity to represent the King of Kings when my initial inclination is to act like the prince of jerks! To be the servant that Christ is; to sacrifice because I love with such reckless disregard for self; to encourage, to celebrate, to give. To love eloquently and with the fullest measure of grace.

Be the presence of Christ on the road, in the grocery store, talking on the phone, having lunch with friends. Christ introduced people to the Father in and through everything that he did, and he introduced the character of the Creator to the human equation of relationships, day-by-day interactions between regular people.

The only way that I can begin to answer the question regarding how my faith has affected my life is to say, honestly and with a lot of disappointment and shame: "Look at the details, the way that I live, and I hope some measure of faithfulness will be evident."

I encounter people at work who will never know Christ if they do not have the opportunity to meet him through the ministry of my living. I want them to understand, every day, that there is a quality to the things that I do and say that invites them to discover more about Jesus.

I am privileged to enter the minds and potentially the souls of thousands of people every week through my newspaper column. It is deliberately presented on the Op-Ed pages because the people who read the more obscure religion section, for the most part, are already Christians. I want all readers, especially nonbelievers, to engage, intellectually, the presence of Christ through my writing, and I want them to feel challenged to give him more serious consideration, to invite the possibility of his truth into their lives.

My wife has a roughly copied quotation pinned to the bookcase behind her desk. It says "The Gospel = the point at which God's Grace intersects our personal experience." My ongoing prayer is that the witness of my life will always be the "God's Grace" part of that equation when other people's experience intersects with mine.

There are many old hymns that beautifully express the idea of God's specific work through the details of our lives. But it is the simplicity of these words from the sixteenth-century *Sarum Primer*, attributed to Augustine (A.D. 354–430), that best define my thoughts regarding faith and life: "God be in mine eyes, and in my looking; God be in my mouth, and in my speaking; God be in my heart, and in my thinking; God be at mine end, and at my departing."

From that perspective, my faith *is* my life.

> Prayer: *Loving Lord, please help us all to carry your presence into this incredibly needy and hurting world through the ministry of our living. We are deeply grateful, yet we feel nervously responsible because of the trust that you place in us. Amen.*

Filling and Pouring, Emptying and Filling

Michael McCormack

(Dedicated to the Presbyterian Church in Bowling Green, Kentucky.)

> *"Be the goal of my pilgrimage, and the rest by the way."*
>
> —*Augustine*

III. Jesus falls the first time*

Can't fall to sleep,
Stop Shepherdsville.
McDee's eager
To sell coffee.
Finally helped awake
By coffee served
Over a billion times.
Dog wants out
But settles and sleeps,
Polite not to rub it in.
Get back driving south
For funeral.

*Editor's note: The sections are excerpts from a larger poem by the author.

Delilah let Samson fall asleep on her lap;
And she called a man,
And had him shave off the seven locks of his head.
He began to weaken,
And his strength left him.

Office was so long
And the Minister sat at the other end.
I didn't know what to say, where
To put my hands. quickly pocketed them.
"I think I want to be a minister."
He sent me north to my home church.
I left his office.
"I'll have to say it all over again."

each step
slower and louder
each moment
longer and hotter
each second
body weaker
beginning to fail
slowly ground moving up
and side and
    fall.
and boy with the rope around your waist pulling you up,
    others angry at your weakness,
others satisfied you failed.
cross-heavy, you pulled up and stand, face stoic and
    helped up.
rest over, your way continues, slow and loud.
o lord christ, i am not worthy to be called by your name
i am empty
fill me for this journey
fill me with your self-emptying love
fill me with the strength to follow you
in the way of the cross.

IX. Jesus falls a third time.

Tennessee winding roads,
Twist, disappear,
Reappear and we never
Found that Unitarian church
In Kingsport. Stopped at
"Awful House" instead.
Brown booths, sheened table.
Over breakfast, worked up
Courage to tell Will
"I want to be a minister."
"Cool," he said. "Not for me,
But cool, Mac."
Still remember his kindness,
More than any friend at college
Gave me a graced moment.
We sat, eating silent toast
And I felt welcomed.

Our steps are made firm by the Lord,
When he delights in our way;
Though we stumble,
We shall not fall headlong,
For the Lord holds us by the hand.

Driving past
Abraham Lincoln's
Historic Brown Sign.
Poet's president.
Sandberg, Whitman loved you.
Don't know you well, myself.
Remember the small cabin,
Tall legs, theater box,
Small gun, your death.
If you had known, perhaps
You'd kiss your wife more.
Maybe not.

I sip my coffee, thankfully.
Never know: last sip,
Last kiss, last fall, last mile.

because you fall, lord, i am able to stand
because you humiliate yourself before the world, lord, i
    can stand
because you take the form of a slave, lord, i stand to serve
    the world you died to save
o lord christ i am not worthy to be called by your name
i am empty
fill me for this journey
fill me with your self-emptying love
fill me with the strength to follow you
in the way of the cross.

In Honey Creek

George R. Pasley

In Honey Creek (Iowa),
Between the interstate and the river,
Between vacation and home,
In a family restaurant
Where bikers dined
With their tattooed wives,
I realized:
Poetry is alternative.
Each line of verse
Is found by poets
Between the lines
Of what other people see.

Sometimes We Are David

George R. Pasley

Sometimes we are David,
stealing consecrated bread,
receiving grace
because you look the other way.

And sometimes we are Benjamin,
finding in the grain you give us
a reminder of our sin.

Sometimes our measures overflow,
pressed down and heaped again,
like the five thousand who were fed
on the banks of Galilee

And sometimes you give us
just enough
when just enough will do,
as the widow of Zarephath,
with only one last measure in her jar,
over and over again.

Sometimes you feed us
out of pity—
for was not the cry of Hagar too terrible to bear?

And sometimes out of loyalty
you send the ravens,
for never do you forget.

Each day,
there is manna in the desert,
Each day,
you break another loaf.

Why Do You Write for Children?

Katherine Paterson

After more than a quarter century as a published writer, I know that there are two questions that I will invariably be asked. The first is one asked of all writers: "Where do you get your ideas?" The second peculiar to those of us who write for the young, "But why do you write for children?" Sometimes the emphasis in the question is on the "why," sometimes the "do," more often on "children." I was amused to discover that after I began to win prizes the emphasis quite often fell on the "you." In other words, now that it had been publicly acknowledged that I wasn't writing for children because I lacked the basic skills to write for grownups, surely I could see that my apprenticeship had been served and my diploma presented. Why, then, did I persist in writing for a young audience? When was I going to write a book for "real" people?

It makes me angry, then sad, that we as a society have so little respect for children. The unstated thesis is that children are not to be taken seriously. It follows that anyone who works with or for children only does so because they are not good enough, clever enough, skilled enough to work in the real, the adult world. There is even a hierarchy among those working with the young. Those working with infants are on the bottom rung, then preschool teachers; slightly above them are elementary school teachers, then the junior high teachers, superseded by the high school teachers who can't quite touch the college and university faculty in status even if their pay is higher. It should follow that those working with the very old are at the apex, but, of course, it doesn't. Those in geriatric care are working with persons in their second childhood and thus get booted down to the bottom again.

So why would anyone choose to write for the young? Flannery O'Connor was once asked by a college student why she wrote. "I said, 'Because I am good at it,' and felt a considerable disapproval in the atmosphere."[1] But, as O'Connor goes on to explain, "There is no excuse for anyone to write fiction for public consumption unless he has been called to do so by the presence of a gift. It is the nature of fiction not to be good for much unless it is good in itself."[2]

It is the nature of gifts to be limited. My gift is to write for children. I write fiction for the young "because I am good at it." I am, I believe, one of the world's fortunate people who discovered fairly early on what my gift was and who has had the joy of exercising that gift for most of my adult life. When individuals in the congregations where my husband has served have wondered aloud why his wife isn't pulling her weight as a clergy spouse ought, he has consistently replied, "Katherine has her own calling." It ended the conversation but not the murmuring. For there is still a persistent suspicion among many church people that God does not call someone to write fiction for children. If she insists on writing for kids, why not curriculum? Why not use those gifts of communicating with children directly in the service of the church? Well, I tried. That was how I started out; indeed, a book that I wrote for the Covenant Life Curriculum in 1966 is still in print in a revised edition. But curriculum, it turned out, was not my gift. Story was.

We give lip service to the power of story, we Christians. "I Love to Tell the Story," "Tell Me the Old, Old Story." There is indeed a movement in homiletics (unless it passed on by while my attention was diverted) to cast sermons in story form. But too often in the church, stories for children are cheats, vehicles for the messages we want to impart, not true stories at all. We don't trust fiction. It is too wild, too untamed. It might carry meanings we hadn't approved beforehand. Indeed, another question asked almost as often as the other two is: "What message do you want to convey to children in this book?" "That's not my job," I answer to the distress of the questioner. "My job is to tell the best, the truest story that I can tell. It is the reader's privilege to choose what she or he will learn from reading the book."

There is one parable in the Gospels that I have long been suspicious of. It is the parable of the Sower. In his other parables, Jesus tells the story and leaves the learnings to his listeners. In the parable of the Sower—in which, not incidentally, an alert listener might find various meanings—Jesus, at the disciples' urging, spells out the intended message. Years before I'd heard of the Jesus Seminar I was deeply bothered. Jesus was telling parables. Parables are literally "thrown beside." They leave the business of understanding to the audience. "He that has ears to hear, let him hear." I can't help wondering if the explanation of the parable of the Sower didn't have its seed in some first-century children's sermon.

There is a Sufi parable about a master who told his disciples a story that, if understood, would bring them to a new level of enlightenment. One of the disciples was baffled by the story and asked for an explanation. The master replied, "Suppose you were to go to the market and find a particularly beautiful peach. After you had paid for it, the fruit seller peeled it and ate it and then gave you back the peel and the pit; what would you think?" "But Master," the disciple persisted, "I don't understand." Whereupon the Master repeated the story of the peach.

We find it very difficult to trust children with the whole peach. Which is why we often give them propaganda and call it story. Propaganda has a bad name, but it is not necessarily a bad thing to systematically propagate a given doctrine. Just don't call it a story. To me propaganda is knowing the answer beforehand and seeking to impart it. When I write a book, I am exploring a question for which I do not have an answer. Because I am a storyteller, I explore life's mysteries by means of story.

The questions I ask seem to be the same questions that thoughtful children are asking, though not in the same words. Who am I? Where did I come from, and where am I going? What are human beings that God should be mindful of them? Who is my neighbor? My brother? My sister? My parent? Why did God choose Jacob and reject Esau? Why do the wicked prosper? Why do the righteous suffer? How can the wounded be healed? Why is there death in the world?

When I was twenty I first read Gerard Manley Hopkins's poem titled "Spring and Fall: To a Young Child." It is a poem I've gone back to over and over again, especially since I became a writer for the young.

> Margaret, are you grieving
> Over Goldengrove unleaving?
> Leaves, like the things of man, you
> With your fresh thoughts care for, can you?
> Ah! as the heart grows older
> It will come to such sights colder
> By and by, nor spare a sigh
> Though worlds of wanwood leafmeal lie;
> And yet you will weep and know why.
> Now no matter, child, the name:
> Sorrow's springs are the same.
> Nor mouth had, no nor mind, expressed
> What heart heard of, ghost guessed:
> It is the blight man was born for,
> It is Margaret you mourn for.

People think they are paying me a compliment when they tell me that I don't really write for children. Or they complain as one woman at a seminary event did: "No child could possibly understand your books. They are too intense." Yet just the week before a fifth-grade teacher had sent to me a book report on *The Great Gilly Hopkins*—written, she said, by the "bad boy" of the class. The concluding sentences of the report read, "This book is a miracle. Mrs. Paterson understands exactly how kids feel." Given the choice between the cool understanding of an adult and the passionate heart of a wounded eleven-year-old, I'll take the heart every time.

Hopkins said to me early on that the feelings of children are intense, often more intense than those of us whose hearts have grown older. Writers for children know this, but they also know that they are writing for persons whose experience and language is limited. We want to express for them the truth they feel but cannot or dare not put into words. But in doing so we must heed the advice of Emily Dickinson, who urges us to "Tell all the Truth but tell it slant . . ."

Books are so much better at presenting the truth at a slant than films, television, or, heaven help us, an Internet site. Books don't bombard the reader with images. Readers construct their own images and will only do so from out of their own experience and imagination. Moreover, you can always close a book, and it will wait for you unchanging until you are ready to take it up again. Young readers can take from my story what truths they themselves are ready to find there and let the rest go for later or choose to close the covers and never open them again.

It is this innate wisdom in the child reader—to find in a story what she or he is ready and able to receive—that makes it possible to write for children at all. The warnings are fearful: "If any of you put a stumbling block before one of these little ones who believe in me, it would be better for you if a great millstone were fastened around your neck and you were drowned in the depth of the sea" (Matt. 18:6). I received a letter from an earnest adult quoting this warning. She had found some profanity in *Bridge to Terabithia* and felt a need to tell me that I would be better off with the biblical millstone around my neck than to write such books for the fragile young. Since I take the Bible very seriously, I did not laugh.

Some years ago a woman who was the librarian in a juvenile corrections facility sought me out at a convention. "I work in a detention center for hard-core delinquents," she said. "That doesn't mean shoplifters and runaways. That means murderers and kids who have committed violent crimes. I just want you to know how much our children love your books. The other day a girl brought back a copy of *Gilly Hopkins* to the library. 'This is me,' she said."

This is why I can't clean up my books. If a girl who is in a center for hard-core delinquents can identify with Gilly, then perhaps she can find someone who will be Trotter for her. It seems significant that the dire warning in Matt. 18:6 is followed soon after by the parable of the Ninety and Nine Sheep who are left safe in the fold while the shepherd seeks out the one lost sheep. Isn't it more important for that one child in a Philadelphia prison to find hope in a story than for the book to receive a seal of approval from polite society?

I think well-meaning adults need to realize that the purpose of fiction is not to set examples but, in the words of Barry Lopez, to "sustain us with illumination and heal us. . . . to repair a spirit in disarray."[3] I cannot bend my characters to fit into narrow definitions of virtuous behavior. The disarray in our children's spirits is not healed or illumined by perfect role models. Confronted with perfection children feel judged and condemned. Moreover, characters without sin are lies. Surely God is not honored by lies.

There are children who live in safe, healthy, nurturing homes with two loving parents, but they are in the minority today even in our own rich country. Perhaps they have always been, and we are just more aware of it. At any rate, as a writer for today's children, I need to think of the vast majority of my audience as deprived. Some are economically deprived, some intellectually and educationally deprived, some emotionally deprived, but even the children of the best of families are all too often spiritually deprived.

I find it disturbing that many adults feel that technology is the panacea for most of the deprivations of childhood. The argument is made that hooking every classroom in America to the Internet will "level the playing field" for our nation's young.

I think it is vital that we who regard ourselves as People of the Book and who honor the creative power of the Word look carefully at what in our enthusiasm for technology we are depriving our children of.

As I read Sven Birkett's eloquent book, *The Gutenberg Elegies*,[4] I realized that children growing up being bombarded by the fragmented images of MTV and the overload of constantly shifting information from the Internet are being deprived in three dangerous ways. The first is in the loss of a rich, subtle, and varied language. The more poverty stricken the child's language, the more superficial his or her thinking will be. Second, our children are being deprived of a sense of history—of the movement from past to present and the many layered riches that each age and civilization piles upon another. In an electronic world nothing is valued or real but the moment. Everything is here and now. And third, our children are being deprived of a private self. I do not lament the growth of community. But the electronic community cannot be thought of as community in the biblical sense. When Paul writes of the oneness of the church, he uses the image of the human body where each member is different and therefore each is vital to the health of the whole. Without the language to think in, with no notion of a God who works through human history, nor any sense of a cloud of witnesses to guide them, how will our children find wisdom? How will they grow their souls? How can they create a nurturing and imaginative community of mature, variedly gifted members?

A book, unlike television, demands the total engagement of its audience. Unlike the Internet, a book consists of words in lines upon a page that take time to read, comprehend, and ponder. The reader is not bombarded with information and images; he or she moves through the text, composes his or her own images and draws his or her own conclusions on the information presented. A reader must invest time and thought and energy in the process and in turn is given all the time he or she wishes. Out of this slow and labor-intensive effort, the reader learns and grows, intellectually, to be sure, but also emotionally and spiritually.

The rich language of the Bible, the historical sweep of its narrative, the vividness and truth of its portrayal of humankind, and its prevailing theme of God's love for not only God's people but for each person and every sparrow, set before the writer of fiction a vision of what a book can do for a reader. And the Bible also serves to warn us of what will be lost when books become obsolete, words debased, and the experience of the past forgotten. We who are People of the Book must not deprive our children of books, of language, or of history. Society as a whole will find us irrelevant; the world, after all, is roaring past in another direction. But even if at times I feel that we who write for today's children are leaning into a gale-force wind, I keep working. I believe children need words, imagination, and story almost as much as they need food, clothing, and shelter.

There is one final reason for working with and for children. It is to learn from them.

> At that time the disciples came to Jesus, saying, "Who is the greatest in the kingdom of heaven?" And calling to him a child, he put him in the midst of them, and said, "Truly, I say to you, unless you turn and become like children, you will never enter the kingdom of heaven." (Matt. 18:1–3 RSV)

In Mark the story of Jesus welcoming the children is followed almost immediately by the story of the rich young ruler. "How hard," Jesus says, "it will be for those who have wealth to enter the kingdom of God!" As opposed, it would seem, to children, who get a free pass. We are inclined to think of riches in relation to material wealth, but if we put the story of Jesus blessing the children side by side with the story of the rich young ruler, perhaps riches are all those valued accretions of adulthood—status, respect, education, even physical size—precisely those things that no child has clinging to him or her. The very reason we do not take children seriously, their lack of power, is the very reason they are scampering unhampered through the Pearly Gates while we are still trying to worm our way through the slits. We do well to stick around children then, for if we would enter the kingdom we must first learn from them how to live.

We Are Earthlings

John C. Purdy

*W*e are earthlings, you and I. We were made from the earth; we were made for the earth. Our future is bound up with the future of the earth, just as surely as its future is bound to ours.

Go out of doors. Take off your shoes, find a patch of ground that is bare, and stand on it. Look around at the trees, the grass, the birds, the sky. You are not rooted in the ground like a tree; you can walk on the surface of the earth. But when you lift your right foot to walk, the left foot presses against the ground with twice the force. Look at the birds; they can fly, you cannot. If you leap into the air, you will quickly return to earth. And where it is soft and yielding, you will sink into it. You were made for the earth.

You were also made from the earth. Scripture says, "In the day that the Lord God made the earth and the heavens . . . the Lord God formed man from the dust of the ground, and breathed into his nostrils the breath of life; and the man became a living being" (Gen. 2:4b, 7). And from that same ground God caused trees to spring forth—fruit-bearing trees, which enabled the earthling to live. The Bible says that God breathed life into us, but also that God planted a garden, that we might continue to live. Our beginning was not in a forest or desert, but in a watered garden.

Before leaving his father's Wisconsin farm, conservation-ist John Muir climbed a favorite hill and wrote of what he observed:

> The highest point commands a landscape circle of about one thousand square miles, composed of ten or twelve miles of the Fox River, Lake Puckawa and five or six nameless lit-tle lakes—marsh and woodland exquisitely arranged and joined—and about two hundred hills, and some prairie. Ah! these are the gardens for me! There is landscape gardening! While we were there, clouds of every texture and size were held above as flowers and moved about as needed, now increasing, now diminishing, lighter and deeper shadows and full sunshine in small and great pieces, side by side as each portion of the great garden required. A shower, too, was guided over some miles that required watering. The streams and lakes and rains and clouds in the hand of God weighed and measured myriads of plants coming into live, each leaf receiving its daily bread—the infinite work done in calm effortless omnipotence.[1]

From day one, God and earth and humankind have been joined together like interlocking rings. God is not our Creator with-out being also the Creator of the heavens and the earth; God is not Creator of heaven and earth without being also our Creator. "Religion binds the whole cosmos starting from above; ecol-ogy binds the whole cosmos from below," avowed Dean James Morton of New York's Cathedral of St. John the Divine.[2]

Mother Earth

If we were made from the earth, may we not claim the earth as Mother? Is this not how each of us came into the world—made in the womb, of the very stuff of our mother's body? Indeed, the earth is our Mother: Once humankind issued from Her; once we were fashioned from Her.

Hopis believe that Mother Earth lives underground by a huge lake. In the floor of their ceremonial kivas is a little hole, called a *sipapu*. When they conduct their rituals, they uncover the *sipapu;* this allows Mother Earth to listen in and to be assured that the right things are being done. Then She will do Her part to ensure that rain and plants and animals do their part to nourish and sustain the Hopis.

In the Genesis story, however, God is not Father in the same way that Earth is Mother. God did not generate us; rather, God fashioned us from the dust of the earth. James Weldon Johnson sang:

> Up from the bed of the river
> God scooped the clay;
> And by the bank of the river
> He kneeled him down;
> And there the great God Almighty
> Who lit the sun and fixed it in the sky,
> Who flung the stars to the most far corners of the night,
> Who rounded the earth in the middle of his hand;
> This Great God,
> Like a mammy bending over her baby,
> Kneeled down in the dust
> Toiling over a lump of clay
> Till he shaped it in his own image;
> Then into it he blew the breath of life,
> And man became a living soul.[3]

We are earthlings, not godlets. Angels were made for heaven; we were made for earth. This is where our past, present, and future are played out. In the end there may indeed be a new heaven and a new earth—but still, an earth. For as Robert Frost avowed in "Birches":

> Earth's the right place for love;
> I don't know where it's likely to go better.

Despoilers or Developers?

But everything on earth has not gone well. Earthlings have never agreed how to honor Mother Earth. We Americans in particular have a long history of disagreement. In 1653 Edward Johnson could count it as a Providential work that "a remote, rocky, barren, bushy, wild-woody wilderness" had been transformed into "a second England for fertileness." Yet two centuries later, Henry David Thoreau would confide in his journal, "Is it not a maimed and imperfect nature that I am conversant with?" Johnson saw how a once-wild New England had been tamed and developed; Thoreau saw what humans had done to despoil the same land.[4]

In *Travels with the Archdruid*, John McPhee describes a 1970 float trip down the Colorado River with David Brower and Floyd Dominy—the spiritual descendents, respectively, of Thoreau and Johnson. "The Archdruid" is McPhee's affectionate name for Brower, longtime head of the Sierra Club. Perhaps only John Muir did more in the twentieth century to fight the developers. And who did more to tame our rivers and develop our waste places than Floyd Dominy, head of the U.S. Bureau of Reclamation?

Those two represent powerful forces that today have opposing views of our relationship to the earth: Some would let the rivers run wild and free to the ocean; others look at the same flow of water and imagine the electric power that could be generated if it were dammed. But neither view denies that we are the earth's as much as the earth is ours. "All things are tied together," an elderly Mayan observed. "When you cut a tree you must ask its forgiveness, or a star will fall from the sky." At least once in every decade a star falls from the sky to remind us that we are earthlings, not gods.

In the summer of 1993 there were titanic floods in the American Midwest. Rains right out of the story of Noah caused the Mississippi and Missouri rivers—and their tributaries—to overflow levees and banks. Millions of acres of farmland were inundated; whole towns were swept away; roads, buildings, trees, silos, cattle, house trailers, barns were destroyed. And all this in a region where a vast network of dams and levees had been built to contain and control the waters.

In 1986 in what was then the Soviet Union a nuclear energy plant at Chernobyl exploded. Its impact dwarfed accidents such as the one at Three Mile Island in Pennsylvania. Dozens were killed; hundreds were sickened; an entire city was left a ghost town; nuclear dust drifted over hundreds of miles. A permanent cloud of doubt and suspicion hangs over every nuclear energy plant in the world.

In 1973 the embargo imposed by the oil-producing nations of the Organization of the Petroleum Exporting Countries (OPEC) forced the developed world to face a terrible reality: Oil, upon which the industrial world depends as its primary source of energy, is a finite resource. Modern civilization rests upon a foundation that is gradually, but inevitably, disappearing. Every time you back your car out of the garage, you are eating into your grandchildren's inheritance.

In 1962 a book as potent as any bomb was published: Rachel Carson's *Silent Spring*. It exposed an entire nation to the dreadful consequences of the unlimited use of synthetic chemicals to control insects and other pests. Each generation ought to read the fable that introduces *Silent Spring*. Carson writes of a town in middle America where people once lived in harmony with the environment. It is an idealized portrait of rural life, with vivid descriptions of the fields and farms and fauna. Then, Carson says, something akin to an evil spell settled on the town and the fields. There were several unexplained deaths among adults and children; livestock mysteriously sickened and died; birds stopped singing; bees deserted the orchards; the fish in the streams died. All of this was traceable to a white powder that had fallen on everything several weeks before. The people had poisoned themselves with a pesticide.[5]

We live as fellow creatures in a world that God made. From time to time we may ignore that fact—blinded by the grandeur of human accomplishments. But we cannot long ignore it; some star will fall from the sky to force our recognition.

Is global warming such a warning? Disturbed by such phenomena, Bill McKibben wrote in *The End of Nature:*

> By the end of nature I do not mean the end of the world. The rain will still fall, and the sun will still shine, though differently than before. When I say "nature," I mean a certain set of human ideas about the world and our place in it. But the death of these ideas begins with concrete changes in the reality around us, changes that scientists can measure. More and more frequently, these changes will clash with our perceptions, until our sense of nature as eternal and separate is finally washed away, and we see all too clearly what we have done.[6]

What we have done, McKibben goes on to assert, is to have built a greenhouse, where once there bloomed a wild garden. But according to the narrative in Genesis, chapters 2 and 3, nature never was a wild garden—separate and independent from humankind. From the very beginning—in the mind and intention of the Creator—earth and earthlings were interdependent. The Bible allows for Mother Earth; but for Mother Nature, never!

What of Evolution?

How does all of this square with Evolution? According to the evolutionary story, humans did indeed emerge from the earth. In some form of life, our antecedents crawled up on land out of the sea. Maybe they crawled into the sea before they crawled back out. But they—we—emerged out of the stuff of the earth. We did not drop down from the sky; nor were we hatched from angel eggs. We were made from the dust of the earth. As such creatures, we are mortal. We do not go on forever. In the scriptural garden that God planted was a tree that had fatal consequences:

> And the LORD God commanded the man, "You may freely eat of every tree of the garden; but of the tree of the knowledge of good and evil you shall not eat, for in the day that you eat of it you shall die. (Gen. 2:16–17)

And when we die, we return to the earth from which we came: ashes to ashes, dust to dust. Once we did not exist; now we exist as flesh and blood, a complex arrangement of chemicals; someday we shall die and cease to be more than separated molecules. Still, we remain part of the earth. Matter can neither be created nor destroyed.

One lovely spring morning in the high desert country of the Southwest, I participated in the scattering of the ashes of a friend. Acting on her expressed wish, we went to a lonely hill. There each of us took some of her ashes in our left hand, and in the right hand some cornmeal. As directed by our Native American mentor, we each went off by ourselves and thought about our friend: We asked her to forgive us for any wrongs done to her; we forgave her for any wrongs she might have done us. Then we scattered the ashes and the cornmeal. There was no thought that she had disappeared, simply because the particles no longer formed a human being. As our Zia guide said to us as we reassembled: "Now she is one of the Ancient Ones." She is still part of the earth and heavens, though not in any form that we can describe. The ongoing history of heaven and earth still includes her.

Made for Mutuality

But "ashes to ashes, dust to dust" is only part of our story. Not only were we made for the earth and from the earth; we were also made of and for the other human being. Genesis tells of the creation of woman. She was not made from the dust of the earth, but rather out of a rib taken from man. The animals all were made from the ground. Not the woman. The relationship of man and woman is profoundly different from that of humans to animals. Man and woman are equal partners, bone of each other's bone and flesh of each other's flesh.

There can be no thought of dominance or mastery of the man over the woman, as there is with humans and the animals. Mutuality, not mastery, is God's intended relationship. When a man abuses his wife we are wrong to accuse him of bestiality. The man who beats his wife is not behaving like a beast. For not even the beasts of the field wantonly abuse their mates—unless they have become crazed or rabid. The man who assaults his wife is treating her as though she were a beast, which is worse than the bite of a dog gone mad.

But why should people turn beastly toward one another? According to the Genesis narrative, the creation of human beings was a risky business. "God does not play at dice," insisted Albert Einstein. Perhaps not. But God certainly gambled in making man and woman. The serpent came to the woman and caused a small worm of doubt to grow in her mind. "Did God say, 'You shall not eat from any tree of the garden?'" (Gen. 3:1b). Note that it is not the man whom the serpent approaches, but the woman. She must rely on the truthfulness of what the man has told her; it was not God's veracity that the serpent questioned, but that of her partner. Whom should the woman believe, the man or the snake? She looked at the tree, saw that it was good to eat and that it might make her wise. She trusted her eyes and her intuition—and ate. And the man trusted her—and he ate. And now the fateful consequences. When God saw what they had done, God drove them from the garden. They could no longer reach out and take food from the trees. They must plow and plant and wait for the harvest. They were now dependent on the earth from which they had been made; they were dependent on its fertility, upon the rains that fell upon it, and upon the seeds that might or might not sprout and produce edible fruit. Was God's action too severe? Put yourself in God's place. Would you simply forgive the humans their presumption? Children are treated like that: When they reach out for something too "adult" for them, they are reprimanded. But they are allowed to remain in the garden, that is childhood. We never grant them freedom as a punishment—only as a reward.

Once the earthlings had eaten of the forbidden tree, God had to create a new future for them. Because the man and woman refused to live in the innocence of childhood, God chose to treat them as adults. Henceforth they could look after themselves. Aldo Leopold, noted ecologist, wryly observed: "There are two spiritual dangers in not owning a farm. One is the danger of supposing that breakfast comes from the grocery, and the other is that heat comes from the furnace."[7]

Writing of her childhood in western Illinois, Mary Austin speaks of the Garden as "the secret place in your mind where you go when you don't like the place where you are." But in the Genesis narrative the man and the woman are not allowed to remain as children. Nor are we. There may have been a time—much nearer to day one than to the present—when God was like a parent and earthlings were like children in a watered garden. But that past is closed to us. We were sent out of the Garden of Eden; we were set to tilling the ground. We were forced to become responsible adults.

All portrayals of the earth as a garden are, in some sense, infantile. They are attempts to escape from the place of responsibility where we find ourselves—where breakfast does not come from the grocery, nor heat from the furnace—and where we have to till the ground to make it yield sustenance.

In the nineteenth century the so-called Mountain Man lived in splendid solitude with an Indian wife, taking from the wilderness everything he needed to live. But he was a little boy playing at being Noble Savage. Fleeing to the mountains of the West was a temporary solution to a problem as old as Genesis. But the West was no Eden. Earthlings cannot get back to the Garden.

So?

Yet the story of the man and woman in the Garden of Eden is one we must not forget, for it firmly establishes who God is in relationship to humankind: God is our Creator, who made us out of the dust of the earth. God and the earth are integral to our present and our future. Also, God made us in mutuality. We cannot find wholeness in relationship to the earth and animals alone, only with other human beings. Such are both our nature and our destiny.

In My Granny's House:
A Recollection

J. Barrie Shepherd

*B*anished to the spare room under the eaves because of a heavy head cold, I was lying awake at 5 A.M., trying to decide whether I could get up and go downstairs without awakening the rest of the family. Suddenly my attention was captured by something almost like lightning flashing across that darkened space. While I puzzled, it happened again and I realized that I was seeing light from the headlamps of passing cars, reflecting from the windowpanes behind my head and glancing round the angles of the ceiling before vanishing toward the city with the early morning traffic. All at once I was back, forty years ago and more, at Granny's house in Scotland where, on my made-up bed on the couch in the front room, I had lain many an evening tracing the self-same phenomenon as cars sped past on their way between Edinburgh and Glasgow.

I don't remember what I thought of those bright glittering beams; whether I imagined they were speeding feys, darting wizard's glances (no lazer guns back in those days); but I do know their swift traverse of the shadowed dark intrigued me as I cuddled down and waited for sleep. My Granny's house was like that. Filled with unfamiliar sights and smells, sounds and flavors, which set it apart as a quite different place—

116

another level of existence really—from the usual, ordinary stuff that made up everyday reality for me.

It was a tiny dwelling place—75 The Gardens, Broxburn—what they used to call in Scotland, "A But and Ben." The "But and Ben" had just two rooms: the "But," in which the family lived, ate and slept; and the "Ben" being the "sitting room," the place kept nice for visitors and the like. When we came to visit, Dad, and/or Mum and I slept "ben the room": parents in the fancy double bed and I, sometimes with my younger brother, Dick, on a long, thin, horsehair-stuffed Edwardian sofa with a cushion and wooden railing along the back, through which we would peek and pretend to be peering through prison bars.

I don't remember too much more about that room except that in one corner there was the "press"—a closet in which the best china was stored—and at the fireplace, just inside the fender, a shiny black pottery cat, playing with a lovely bright green ball. How I wished I could pull the ball away and play with it myself, or maybe roll it back and forth to tease the cat into some game or other.

In the other room, the "But" where Granny and Grandpa lived, my memories are more detailed. There was the old-fashioned fireside, the kind they call an "inglenook" in sentimental songs. It had a grate for the coal to burn, a hob for kettle or cooking pots, and an oven at the side in which Granny did her baking. Beneath the window, which looked out across the tiny garden onto the main Edinburgh road, was "the well" and the sink. The well was one cold water tap which—along with the indoor toilet—constituted all the running water they had, as far as I recall. I can still feel the warm tingling of nose and ears after my early morning wash there with strong, clean-smelling soap and a good coarse towel.

Beside the fireplace was a big armchair in which I could usually find my grandfather, when he wasn't out walking his dog, Seesee, on their daily four- or five-mile constitutional.

He read the newspaper and smoked a pipe—a series of pipes, all with silver caps on them—and seemed to talk more to his pet Pekingese than to any of us. I remember helping him wash the little beast (it was not very friendly to youngsters) in the "wash hoose" that belonged to the big house next door, and that smell of old wet dog trails across my memory to this day.

The wall opposite the hearth was almost entirely occupied by the "box bed," a furnishing unique—as far as I know—to Scotland. It was simply a double bed immovably built into a large recess in the wall, and curtained off from the rest of the living area. Under the "box bed" all kinds of seldom-used items were hidden away.

Along the back wall of the house, directly opposite the window, was a massive oaken chest of drawers in which they must have stored most of the possessions they had managed to accumulate or preserve over fifty years of marriage and the raising of seven children. Another "press" in the far corner near the fire served as both pantry and kitchen cabinet. My baby sister, Kaye, when she had just begun to walk, used to love to totter to this press and carry out handful after handful of flatware, which she then proceeded to dump in the lap of her grandfather, much to the old man's chuckling delight. I remember my amazement at learning he could actually laugh!

With such limited storage space, the provision of food was a daily activity, made easier for an elderly couple by the various horse-drawn vans that would stop right at the door. There was the milkman, of course, and the butcher's and greengrocer's vans. My favorite was the co-op bakery van, which glided in on rubber tires with its delectable load of scones, teabread, iced and cream cakes, as well as the more pedestrian trays of morning rolls, plain bread, and pan loaves.

I loved to savor the assorted scents of that experience. There was the strong, clear tang of the horse, with oats in the nosebag, the worn leather of the harness, the warm rich manure fresh on the street. Inside the van you stood upright in the center with racks on either side and overhead too, racks crammed with wooden trays that held the marvelous selection of baked goods that every baker in those days turned out as his stock in trade. How I wished that Granny could have been a bit more adventurous in her buying at the baker's van, but even if the will had been there, I suspect the finances were not. As with all purchases from the co-op, Granny paid with plastic tokens, exotic, brightly colored coinage, some of it hexagonal or with—marvel of marvels—a hole in the middle. These tokens were issued by the Cooperative Societies in Scotland in place of money and, I believe, were purchased at a discount as one of the benefits of membership.

It's been well over forty years since I was in that house, yet my memories of it are full and fond. Above all else I remember it as a warm and welcoming place, a spot where wonderful things might be about to happen, a place whose very atmosphere was pervaded by the kind and gentle personality who had made it her last earthly home. When I recite the Shepherd's psalm—the twenty third—and ponder in the last verse about what it might mean, might feel like, to dwell in God's house forever; when I ask myself what Jesus had in mind when he spoke about his Father's house with its "many mansions"; my mind and soul find themselves wandering back to 75 The Gardens, Broxburn, to Granny Shepherd's house and that genuine delight I knew in all my visits there; to that sense that I have known, and pray will know again of being completely at home.

Strange what sudden light in darkness will provoke, stir up, and quieten down within the tossing, turning human soul!

My Education

Martha Evans Sparks

I was six years old in June. I had known all summer that this day was coming. We all knew it. Billy next door, and Gene across the street, and Betty Jane at the end of the block, all of us knew the dreadful day was coming when the school bell tolled for us. First grade began the day after Labor Day on the first Tuesday in September. You couldn't dawdle over breakfast or sit in the top of the cherry tree half the morning anymore.

First grade was different from kindergarten. You had to go every day, it lasted until the middle of the afternoon, and from what the bigger kids said, school went on the rest of your life. There were *eight* grades, could you believe it? And then a mysterious thing called high school after that. But that was in another building and too far in the future to worry about now. I had enough trouble thinking about first grade and the major loss of freedom imminently descending upon me.

Mother said she would go with me the first day. She didn't really have to. I knew perfectly well where the school was, and in our little town everybody walked everywhere.

The day dawned, one of those warm, golden days of late summer common in Kentucky. Dreary old meteorologists say it is only sunlight refracted by dust in the air. But they are wrong. God is shaking down the golden light in particles through a sieve. It was just the kind of day to ride my tricycle up and down the gentle slope of our North Maple Avenue hill. Instead, I was about to start on the long road to literacy.

By coincidence, we had a houseguest. His name was Professor Fisher, a dignified gentleman traveling alone. I had heard of Professor Fisher for all of the few years that a six-year-old has had continuous memory. He had been headmaster, chancellor, president, whatever they called him—how should I know?—where my mother went to college. It was a girls' school small enough to afford opportunity for students to develop friendships with faculty. The school's rules of behavior for the young ladies sounded draconian to me. But Mother had been happy there, graduating second in her class, and had developed a firm friendship and vast respect for this man from her father's generation. Like my grandfather, Professor Fisher was a Methodist minister by training, a Victorian gentleman, genial in company, with rock-ribbed integrity and an uncompromising heart of love for his God and compassion for all people.

As was the household custom, after breakfast we went into the living room for family prayers. When the family was alone, my father always read a chapter from the Bible and Mother prayed. We got down on our knees for the prayer. Nobody worried about whether the children were bored by this. We weren't; it did not occur to us. This was the way mornings started. I assumed it was the same in every household in the entire world.

On this morning, as a mark of honor and respect the guest was asked to lead the prayer. I presume he made a usual sort of prayer, with praise and petitions for the kind of things appropriate in such a setting; I have no memory of it. The prayer was going along when suddenly I heard Professor

Fisher say, "And Lord, we ask your blessings on this child who today begins her educational career."

I was startled. Did he mean me? He was an august presence. I had not supposed he was aware of my existence. I peeked through my fingers. His head was tilted back, his silver hair highlighted in the shafts of golden light from the open door behind him.

"Bless her, Lord. Quicken her mind. Make her able to learn. To the end of her education, keep her in your care, capable of doing the work required."

Timid, innocent child that I was, I knew I was seeing something more in that man's face than the glow of late-summer Kentucky sunshine. I didn't tell anybody about peeking. How could I make an adult understand the way my small spirit leapt within me in response to his prayer? I had never heard of the *shekinah* glory of the Lord.

"Give her an interest in learning, help her to complete a good education. And give her a thirst for acquaintance with you."

The prayer ended. Mother and I left for school with my new tablet and pencil. I never mentioned the experience to anyone, even when we heard several years later that Professor Fisher had died.

But now and again, as the years came and went, what psychologists call an eidetic image of what I had seen between my fingers that morning shimmered in my mind's eye. I could see again a snapshot, an exact visualization of that man's saintly face turned up to God and God's light returning the glance. The same sense of holy quiet revisited me, and with it the inner peace, the reality of God's presence reminding me that I can do all things through Christ who strengthens me (Phil. 4:13). It came in sixth grade when we all puzzled over how to find the volume of a sphere (like anybody wanted to know, I thought). It returned in ninth grade when I confronted Latin grammar, and was there in college with its mountains of reading.

Fast-forward to graduate school. Again it was summer. My little room on the top floor of an un-air-conditioned dormitory at the University of Kentucky was hot. I threw myself across the bunk bed. How could I do it? I was finishing up a master's degree in experimental psychology. I had to study for final examinations in the course work, finish writing my thesis, and prepare for the oral defense of it before a not-particularly-friendly faculty committee. I knew my faithful mother was praying for me. I deeply appreciated it. But as I lay there, again I saw in my mind's eye that godly man's face, tilted back, reflecting the presence of the God he loved and served. The sense of peace returned, and his prayer once more echoed gently inside my head. "Make her able to learn. To the end of her education, keep her in your care, capable of doing the work required."

Does God answer seventeen-year-old prayers, uttered by persons long since gone into God's presence? Undoubtedly, because I got all of that work done, passed the oral examination, and received the degree on time at the August commencement.

When we pray, it is usually for the local and the immediate. Bless Mrs. Smith who is sick. Bless Mr. Jones who needs a job. Bless me because I have this decision to make. These are good, reasonable prayers. God hears and answers. Mrs. Smith gets well, Mr. Jones finds a job, and I decide something. We thank the Lord and move on. But sometimes does one of God's saints have the presence of mind to pray for the long haul? And the amazing thing is that God seems to hear for the long pull.

Although the Bible assures us that God will remember the divine covenant with Abraham forever (Ps. 105:6–8), I am startled by God's attention to the details of the lives of ordinary individuals like me. The omnipotent Lord of the universe keeps me in mind, as if hearing again and deferring to a prayer uttered in my childhood and using it to bless me again years later.

Many persons have prayed for me, and I am grateful to each of them. But it was Professor Fisher who enlarged my concept that our faithful God honors prayers, not only in the immediate but also in perpetuity. It is his gift of faith to me, and it keeps giving and giving over the decades. My mother and my father have now joined her old mentor on the echoless shore. When I, too, pass that way, as we all shall, perhaps there will be an opportunity to thank Professor Fisher for his very real contribution to my education.

A Grief Reobserved

David Steele

The Hyphen

*C*handler snickers as I drive tentatively up this street and down that one searching in vain for the college where my father once was president. He is willing to concede the town has grown, its traffic patterns shifted in my twenty years' absence, but surely by now I should recognize something familiar. Didn't I live here once?

No. This is the town where my parents lived after I left the nest. I visited them here on holidays and vacations. The town is theirs, not mine. Here were their friends, their favorite restaurants, the places that interested them, the things they loved to do. I have always seen the town through their eyes. Now that they are gone, I am blind.

By accident we came upon the sign that points our way to the school. Voilà, we are among familiar buildings. Here is the library and old main; the football field is over there. I park in front of the president's home. Across the street must be the dormitory named for Dad.

It was a thoughtful retirement gesture, putting Dad's name on that building. His years at the helm were good ones for the college. The school was healthy. The trustees chose to honor him in this way. Dad was quietly pleased.

Mother was proud as punch and quite verbal, within the family. She hoped her sons appreciated this honor shown their father. I certainly was impressed. In those days I thought getting your name on a room, like the Steele Fellowship Hall, would be a big deal. Wow! Dad had made it on a building. It was a visible sign that he had done something that his life had mattered. A slice of immortality.

We cross the street and, sure enough, here is the dorm. On the grass in front of the building is a large sign. There in big letters is my father's name, *along with someone else's.* My father has been hyphenated! Two names separated by a hyphen now grace that building sign.

Immortality turns out to be more transient than it is billed. It appears once we have shuffled off this mortal soil there is the distinct possibility of hyphenation. (Commas next?) The dorm sign reads like the name of a contemporary married couple. Did Dad know this other person—or is he coupled with a stranger?

All sorts of interesting scenarios play themselves out in my mind. My father, the hapless "hyphenee" knew/knew not his "hyphener." They were best friends/couldn't stand each other. They . . .

I am confident we could find someone on campus who knows the facts about that hyphen. The mystery undoubtedly has a logical explanation once the facts are known. But we've no time for fact gathering, and for now I resist turning that wonderful hyphen-sign into just another fact. More facts, I don't need. Stories are more nourishing.

Funny thing about immortality: it doesn't last very long.

The Golf Clubs

Chandler and I are barreling cross country. Our schedule calls for no more than a six-day drive. We cannot linger at this Midwestern college. But there is time to pause before the chapel and remember.

There we bid Dad farewell. Jim, Mother, and I sat in those front seats and heard the tributes, prayed the prayers, and as the tears ran down sang the hymn he loved: "God of our life, through all the circling years, we trust in thee. . . ."

It's been twenty years, but at this place those memories still carry great emotional freight, more than I expect. I know better. Love never ends. Why should grief?

Then I remember the golf clubs. They were top of the line—Arnold Palmer Specials, complete with a personal letter of greeting from Arnie himself. Dad was given these clubs at his retirement dinner. The clubs considerably upgraded the tools of Dad's bogey career. He used them with pride, cared for them lovingly.

Those clubs are the first things I notice when I arrive at the house for the memorial service. He died while I was five thousand miles away. There was no chance to say goodbye. I am drawn to these tangible things my father had touched so often in my presence.

Whenever we got together, Dad and I played golf. There on the golf course I knew him best. There we related horizontally. I recall him sighing as we walked toward the eighteenth green at the Pali Course; perhaps it was the last time we played—"I think God's final task for me is to take care of your mother," he said, but did not elaborate. I supposed it to be a generic comment.

Now as we plan his memorial, I understand Dad's specificity. It is clear Mother is not able to handle funeral arrangements by herself. She is "forgetful" and has been so for some time, according to her closest friends. Dad has handled the details of her life so well that many are not aware of her handicap. Mother will need our help in the days and years ahead as Dr. Alzheimer's syndrome purloins her memories.

I am drawn to those golf clubs. I swing them one by one, pitch balls in the back yard, putt on the rug. I remember those dawn golf games.

Dad woke at first light nearly every day. In the summer that came pretty early. In his latter years he figured out what to do at dawn. He'd leap out of bed, make a quick cup of coffee, drive to the local country club, and tee off. He could play eighteen holes, shower, breakfast, and be at his desk by 9:00 A.M.

On vacation visits I would sleepily join him at dawn on the links. As we walked those fairways, the early morning dew soaked our shoes. My father was the world champion at putting greens covered with quarter-inch moisture. When my putts ended up yards short, his ball, swirling water a foot high, cozied right up to the cup. My only hope was to hang on until the sun took care of the dew. On dry greens Dad's putting was atrocious.

So as I swing those irons, I realize what I want to do. I want to get up at dawn tomorrow, take these clubs to the golf course, and remember my father on the links he loved so well. I hope his best friend Harvey can join me. The two of them played weekly. I envision Harvey and me walking those familiar fairways, putting dewy greens, sharing Dad memories, telling stories, and mourning together.

It's a perfect idea; I can hardly wait to ask Harvey. When he and his wife drop by to see if we need any assistance, I take him aside: "Harvey, let's you and me play a memorial game of golf tomorrow morning." I elaborate as best I can. I'm sure he'll get the point.

I am mistaken. Harvey shakes his head in disbelief: "Your father is dead and you want to play golf?"

It's not going to work. I drop the idea. We can grieve side by side, Harvey and I, but not together.

The Game

The memorial service for my father is nigh perfect. I cannot conceive of one more fitting. I do not miss the memorial golf game. Harvey is right; it doesn't fit.

I take Dad's clubs back with me to Hawaii, for sentimental reasons of course, but mainly because they are much better than the ones I own. I intend to try them out right away, but the school year is in full swing. I have to run like fury to catch up.

Those clubs languish in my garage for nearly two months before a school holiday gives me a chance for golf. There are several foursomes of us playing at Scofield Barracks. It is November. I stand on the first tee, swing Dad's driver, and whack the ball 230 yards straight down the middle. All right! I don't do this often. These are great clubs!

Thus begins the best nine holes of golf I ever played. After four straight pars I begin to realize something unusual is happening. After eight pars I have it figured out. In some mystical way, I am in touch with my father.

I am conscious of operating on two levels. I am walking the course as usual, admiring good shots, commiserating with my friends over poor ones. All that is perfectly normal; except I am not hitting poor shots!

On another level I am in communion with my father. There is no organ or harp music, no blinding lights, no dialogue. I simply have a sense of companionship, nonvisual, nonverbal, yet real.

For nine holes I have a perfect swing. I don't know where it comes from. It's not mine; certainly not Dad's. My theory is that for a time I am not thinking about my game and hence my muscles are loose and free. I shoot par for nine holes—a feat not equaled before nor since.

I stride confidently to the tenth tee. Alas, my drive is a classic Steele slice. It ends up in the rough behind a tree. Welcome back to Earth, Dave. Your mystic moment is over. I am on my own—with my regular swing. I shoot bogey on the back nine.

So what happened? There on that golf course, probably on the ninth green, I passed through the toughest part of grieving, letting go. I bid Dad *shalom*, wished him well on his new adventure and moved back into my own bogey-filled life.

I'm thinking about this and more as we pull away from the campus and head for Chicago. Chandler notices that I am pensive but does not intrude. I don't tell him about golf clubs and letting go. It's not the sort of thing a person brings up to enliven the conversation.

I will someday. He knows that. We're both content to wait.

Let's Not Be Afraid of Ambiguity

Eva Stimson

*T*he world is full of ambiguity and so is the Christian faith. Should that scare us? I don't think so. *Ambiguous* is defined in the dictionary as "doubtful or uncertain" and "capable of being understood in two or more possible senses." I believe we in the Presbyterian Church (U.S.A.) would be a lot healthier and happier if we acknowledged and learned to celebrate ambiguity.

Perhaps we could start by forcing our vocal chords to utter more often three disarmingly simple but underused words: "I don't know." Let's face it—for most of us reality is becoming more incomprehensible by the minute, and faith does not always provide neat and tidy answers to today's moral, ethical, or technological dilemmas.

Who knows how to stop the fighting in the Middle East—and in the Presbyterian Church? Or why some people are homosexuals, or whether God is best envisioned as male or female? More often than not, we don't know the answers to the raging controversies of the day. So why not just admit it?

There was a time—fairly early in my faith development—when I thought it was my Christian duty to know or at least know where to find the answer to any question of potential

131

cosmic significance. (And it's amazing how many questions can be made to fit into the "cosmically significant" category.) The older I get, the more I realize that certainty is not a virtue. I've seen how few things we really are capable of understanding in this life. Even the Bible, our authoritative guide, is not always crystal-clear.

Don't get me wrong—I'm not a relativist. Heaven forbid! That would be almost as bad as being labeled a heretic or a pagan. And I may have quit the academic track after two master's degrees, but I'm no proponent of intellectual laziness.

I'll readily confess that Jesus Christ is my Savior, and I'm eager to analyze what that means. But I also think the truth behind that confession is much more complex and wonderful than any of us can know. I'm content to postpone until the life to come my expectation of definitive answers and definitions.

I'm finally getting comfortable out here on the threshhold of eternal life, where things are rarely black-and-white, but mostly gray, and the skies are always partly cloudy. I just wish it wasn't so noisy. People around me—Presbyterians in particular—spend so much time shouting at one another that I can hardly hear myself think.

I suggest we post prominently at presbytery and General Assembly meetings these words from 1 Cor. 13:12: "For now we see in a mirror, dimly, but then we will see face to face. Now I know only in part; then I will know fully, even as I have been fully known."

Let's declare a moratorium on polemics and name-calling in the church. We do not have to produce an opinion or position paper in response to every whiff of controversy. If we simply must put pen to paper—or fingers to the computer keyboard—let's write more poetry and fiction. Let's rediscover the power of metaphor.

Jesus frequently answered his critics with enigmatic statements or stories. "Render to Caesar the things that are Caesar's, and to God the things that are God's." It's hard to get more ambiguous than that. And the early creed-writers weren't much better. "God in three persons . . . " Talk about ambiguity!

If we want clarity we should look at Jesus' life. He consistently treated all kinds of people with love, respect, and compassion. What would it take to get those of us who call ourselves Jesus' followers to stop arguing for a few decades and practice love?

I don't know.

Charity Begins at Homes
with Lemonade Stands

Bill Tammeus

Woodstock, Illinois: "You want some lemonade?" the kid hollered at us from across the street. My old street, actually, West South Street, the street on which I spent much of my boyhood, the street on which, as a kid myself, I sold lemonade at a similarly rickety sidewalk stand.

"You're our first customer, and the first customer gets it free," the boy said. My sister and I looked at each other. The look said: How can you beat free?

So we walked across and bellied up to the bar at the corner of South and Hayward streets. Two boys sat (well, sat in the up-and-down ways boys sit) on chairs behind a small table just one house down the sidewalk from the house in which my sister and I grew up. She and I were in town for a visit and were taking a look at the home of our childhood.

I held my cup of free lemonade and took a sip (hoping the kids' parents had made it).

My sister asked them where they lived. They pointed to two houses down Hayward. It was hard to tell which ones they meant. And, anyway, the people we once knew who lived in those houses no doubt were, like us, long gone.

"Do you know what?" I asked the boys.

"What?"

"When I was about your age, I lived in that house right there. And I used to sell lemonade right out here at the edge of this same sidewalk."

"You did?" one boy asked. He seemed intrigued. The other kid was more interested in finding their first paying customer.

"Yes, I did. And one day some high school kids drove up in a car. One of those big boys in the car got out and came up to me and handed me a dollar, but he didn't want any lemonade. He just handed me a dollar and left."

I reached into my pocket and pulled out four quarters.

"Here," I said. "Maybe someday you'll remember this the way I still remember that."

The kid took the money. My sister and I headed up the hill toward our old house. I had waited nearly fifty years to do that, and it felt good.

It's really quite astounding how we remember small acts of unexpected kindness. I have no idea why that high school kid back in the 1950s gave me a whole dollar—quite a prize then. But the experience made me believe what I still believe, which is that sometimes grace—pure, unmerited favor—falls on us, some unimagined gift from an unimagined source.

Sometimes the best of human nature simply pours forth unbidden and unexpected, undoing our cynicism, making us feel foolish for having doubted goodness.

I don't mean to say that such acts of impulsive charity and surprising dispensation make us vulnerable to cheats and knaves because we trust everyone everywhere to behave similarly. But I do mean to say that the teenager who gave me a dollar once at my lemonade stand here helped to create in me the capacity to believe in kindness. If children never experience grace, they often grow up counting the cost of everything and always keeping score.

How lovely life can be—at least for a while, at least with some people—when you don't have to keep score. And that's what small acts of generosity can teach a child.

About one hundred miles south of Woodstock is Streator, Illinois, where my late mother and her sister grew up on a farm. Their parents, my grandparents, were soft-hearted (but sometimes hardheaded) Swedes who, as immigrants with accents, learned how to work hard and become part of the American social fabric. They also knew about grace.

When a visit to my grandparents' ended, we'd head out to the car to go home. And as we shared farewell hugs, Grandpa invariably would give us four kids a dollar each, as Grandma looked on approvingly. Our parents insisted that we not come to expect this largess, and we tried our best to learn that lesson, though sometimes grace leads to expectation, just as repeated acts of mercy can lead us to misinterpret justice as punishment.

But surely that is a risk worth taking. Surely it is better to open up children to the healing and tender balm of generosity than it is to fill their lives with rigid laws demanding an eye for an eye, a tooth for a tooth.

Acts of grace can teach children how to hope, how to love. There are times to teach responsibility, duty, commitment, obligation. But if that's all we teach, we get fettered children who always calculate precise gains and losses, children whose buds never bloom.

From the Back Pew

Jerry L. Van Marter

December, 1995

*B*aptizing two children was the last thing I expected to do when I traveled to Northern Ireland last month.

I went to Belfast to interview church and political leaders about the prospects for peace in a troubled land that had seen twenty-five years of warfare between Catholic and Protestant paramilitaries come to a fragile cease-fire one year ago. Northern Ireland is still a segregated province, with Catholics and Protestants living and working in rigidly defined communities. There is peace but very little harmony.

One evening, Norma McConville, a wonderful Protestant laywoman who works tirelessly for peace, took me to the birthday party of her daughter-in-law. At the party I met Sally, a young mother who had brought her nine-month-old daughter, Clara, to the party because she could not afford a baby-sitter. During the course of our conversation, Sally told me she was very worried about Clara, who was rapidly losing weight. Doctors had been unable to determine what was wrong.

What worried Sally most was that Clara had not been baptized. When I asked why not, Sally said that she was Catholic and her husband was Presbyterian, and in their village of Tandragee the animosity was so strong that neither the Catholic priest nor the Presbyterian minister would baptize the child of a "mixed marriage."

I couldn't believe such a thing and impulsively offered to baptize Clara myself. So the next evening I returned to the scene of the birthday party—this time to baptize Clara.

There's more. Sally showed up with her next-door neighbor, Debbie, who was holding her three-year-old son, Jonathan. Debbie was Presbyterian, her husband Catholic. Same priest. Same Presbyterian minister. Same refusal to baptize a child.

And so in that crowded little cottage in Tandragee, surrounded by a few family and friends, Clara and Jonathan were welcomed into the family of faith. It was one of the most powerful experiences of my life.

Might the Catholic and Presbyterian churches of Northern Ireland be mad at me? Probably. Could the Presbyterian Church (U.S.A.) discipline me? Maybe. I don't care.

To that little congregation in Tandragee, I read from Mark 10: people are bringing their children to Jesus and the disciples try to keep them away. Jesus, indignant, says, "Let the little children come to me; do not stop them; for it is to such as these that the kingdom of God belongs" (v. 14b).

My little children, Luke and Rachel, pray for Clara and Jonathan every night.

Putting the Amazing Back in Grace

Ann Weems

My mother wrote fiction in the breakfast room;
my father wrote sermons in the study;
I wrote poetry in the maple tree . . .
that friend of a tree who gave me sanctuary,
hiding me in generous foliage from the voices
who called me to do homework or dishes . . .
that friend of a tree, who asked nothing, yet . . .
lifted me closer to the stars.
I'm not certain when I first
became enamored of words.
I suspect the fascination came
from the sound before the sight.
Our father and our mother filled our heads
with stories, both secular and sacred.
The words of nursery rhymes
and the words of psalms
embedded themselves within me.
Words . . . glorious words . . . ,
words memorized that live with me still,
words that come unbidden from shadowy
corridors connecting mind and emotions,
words that bring welcome meaning
to the present moment.
Of course, the present moment finds the church

in chaos: splintered, fractious, quarrelsome . . .
an unpleasant place for poets.
The bickering drowns out the cries of the poor.
Our hearts are closed against the poetry of God.
And we are amazed about nothing.
Poets weep because we'd rather be
out searching for stars.
So the question is: What's a nice poet like me
doing in a church like this?

I was born and bred in the Presbyterian briar patch.
I was one of those children who actually
wanted to go to Sunday School.
By the time I was six, I was completely
captivated by the Red Letter Testament.
I read it in my tree.
I read it in the red leather chair
in my father's study, and by flashlight
when I should have been asleep.
Beautiful red letters . . . Beautiful red words . . .
out of the mouth of Jesus. . . .
"Jesus loves me, this I know
for the Bible tells me so."
"Let the little children come unto Me."
So we came, dressed in our best for Jesus,
our nickels clutched in our hands,
our little souls waiting for the Spirit,
our little hearts already given away . . . to Jesus.
We gladly put our nickels in the hand of Jesus.
We knew what the red words said:
"Feed the hungry."
Jesus took our nickels and bought food
for starving children all over the world.
We had learned that
"the Lord loves a cheerful giver."
We gave, and we were cheerful about the giving.
Soon, however, I noticed that not everyone
who went to church was cheerful.

I noticed it, but I didn't understand it.
Didn't they have Red Letter Testaments?
And why were they mad at my father
because he preached about peace?
And why did their faces turn red
when he preached about racial equality?
And why did the angry phone calls
come when he preached against
low wages for the poor?
Why did people make faces
when he preached about loving
people of other faiths?
They said don't preach about poverty,
and don't preach about peace, and
don't preach about loving other people,
not if their skin is another color,
not if their faith is not called Christian.
I was confused because I had
memorized these red words:
"You shall love the Lord your God
with all your heart and with all
your soul and with all your mind.
This is the greatest and the first commandment.
And the second is like it:
You shall love your neighbor as yourself."
If the first commandment is to love the Lord
your God with all your heart, soul, and mind,
and if the second is like it,
then the way to love God is to love
your neighbor as you love yourself.
I figured it out: I didn't love God if
I said something mean to Norvella,
whose skin was black.
I didn't love God if I wouldn't
let Jerome Rosenfeld play with us.
I didn't love God if I wanted to
bomb the Germans, and I didn't love
God if I didn't share my money.

My father said there was something else.
He said he didn't love God
if he didn't love the people who
wouldn't share their money.
He didn't love God if he didn't
love the people who hated Norvella.
He didn't love God if he didn't love
the people who hated Jerome Rosenfeld.
He didn't love God if he didn't love
the people who wanted war.
He didn't love God if he didn't love
the people who were calling him names,
the people who were trying to get rid of him,
the people who did get rid of him.
Then he said he didn't love God
if he didn't forgive them, and
he didn't love God if he didn't
try to reconcile with them.
I didn't know what "reconcile" meant,
but my mother said it meant that
Jesus forgave the people who nailed him
to the cross, and he loved them still.
That sent me to the Red Letter Testament.
Sure enough, in red words Jesus says:
Forgive them, for they don't know
what they're doing.
It was the most astounding thing I'd ever heard!
Forgive the people who nailed him to the cross. . . .
Forgive the people who despised him.
Forgive the people who rejected him.
Forgive the people who denied him.
Forgive the people who abandoned him,
the people who left him all alone.
Forgive the people who nailed him to the cross.
Because of that, my father was supposed
to forgive and love still
the very people who called him names,
the people who turned his life upside down,

the people who told him he wasn't
the kind of preacher they wanted.
I began to feel a little guilty,
because to tell you the truth,
I was mad at Norvella
because she was so bossy,
and as a matter of fact,
I was tired of Jerome Rosenfeld
hanging around all the time,
being so cheerful.
And what was I going to do
to stop that tune from whirling
around in my brain: "Praise the Lord
and pass the ammunition"?
At least I liked giving my money
to Jesus for the starving children,
but I didn't know how far
that was going to get me.
So I wrote a poem, an adjective-laden poem,
about how much I loved Jesus.
I showed it to my mother,
who warned me about being pious.
My mother said she abhorred piosity.
Of course, I didn't have any idea
what that meant.
My brother said it meant she hated
people acting so goody-goody.
"You don't want to be like the Pharisees,"
she said.
Pharisees. . . . What a delicious word!
Pharisees. . . .
But when I found it
in the Red Letter Testament,
I was horrified. Was I a Pharisee?
My own mother had warned me!
Even Jesus was mad at the Pharisees.
I tore up the poem.
All those beautiful adjectives

ended up in the wastepaper basket.
That was just the first time.
When we moved to our new home
and our new church, I felt better.
We had escaped from the Pharisees.
In 1942 I joined the church.
I was eight years old.
When I said Jesus Christ was my
Lord and Savior, something happened
in my little eight-year-old heart.
I was astounded at my good fortune,
amazed that, even though I had Pharisee
tendencies, I could join this church
where these people wanted to hear
my father preach about peace and race
and justice for the poor and cooperating
with people of other faiths.
I was nurtured by this community of faith.
The Presbyterian Church became my home.
About this time I read in my Red Letter Testament
the story of the woman who touched the hem
of Jesus' robe and, because of her faith, was healed.
I wondered why we had to go through
all that quarreling in the other church,
and why I had to be so careful not to be
a Pharisee, when all she had to do
was touch the hem of Jesus' robe.
My father said it was a matter of faith.
He said we were all inheritors of this faith.
It was something like inheriting Great-
Grandfather's money, which we didn't,
but . . . we did inherit our faith.
My father said that God had given us far more
than Great-Grandfather ever could have given.
God had given us Jesus, who calls
the whole world to his table . . .

Jesus who forgives, and loves us still,
even when we, like sheep, have gone astray . . .
even when we despise and reject him,
even when we abandon him. . . .
Over time, I realized that my father
had forgiven the red-faced people
who called him names.
When we saw them on the street,
he would greet them cheerfully.
I could tell he loved them still.
I thought it was amazing!
I prayed to Jesus not to let me grow up
to be a Presbyterian Pharisee.
My mother, the writer and the lawyer,
pointed out that the people who Jesus
chastised were the good church people,
the ones who claimed that they,
and they alone, knew the real truth,
the ones who knew the letter of the law,
but did not act in the spirit of the law.
My father called them hard-hearted.
He said there's no reason why
Christians can't disagree
and hold hands at the same time.
Now, isn't that amazing!?

I attempted another poem.
My mother said that it was better,
but maybe I'd like to go with her
to a writing class. I did and this time,
I tried a poetic short story.
The teacher said it was a perfect
short story, as soon as I scratched
out all the lovely adjectives.
What a temptation it is to string
pretty words across a page and call it poetry.

What a temptation it is to think that
my little kingdom is the Kingdom of God.

I was warned years ago that nobody likes
poetry and certainly nobody buys it!
What worried me then, what worries me
still, is how easily we in the church
forget the poetry of God,
how easily we in the church
extract the amazing from grace,
how easily we turn
Hosanna into ho-hum and
belief into bureaucracy and
righteousness into rules.
Addicted to our agendas,
bound to our budgets, we fail to
remember that the Love of God
is written upon our hearts . . . ,
not in the Book of Order.
When we worship process,
we obliterate poetry.
We cover our eyes and our ears
against the beautiful red words,
the amazing words of the Word.
Jesus told the people to love their enemies,
and the people were amazed.
He told them to have compassion for strangers,
and the people were amazed.
He overturned the tables of the moneychangers,
and the people were amazed.
He told them to pray for those who persecuted them,
and the people were amazed.
He told them to set the captives free,
and the people were amazed.
He broke the rules, and healed on the Sabbath,
and the people were amazed.
While we in the church are spending
our energy on arguing,

who will bind the wounds?
And who will free the oppressed?
And who will feed his sheep?

I'm back in the church down in Tennessee. . . .
Yes, yes, I know: The Presbyterians have
a history of fighting, ... but our faith has a
history of forgiving.

I have reached for rainbows.
I have searched for shalom.
I have shared my family faith stories.
I have knelt in Bethlehem.
I have knelt in Jerusalem.
I have cried my laments in the face of God,
and God has continued to leave
stars where I can find them.
Surely, we in the church have love enough
to disagree and hold hands at the same time!
"He was despised and rejected,
a man of suffering and acquainted with grief."
Who do we say that he is?
Who do we say that he is by the way we live?
"He is the One who was wounded for our transgressions.
By his bruises we are healed.
By his punishment we are made whole."

I don't know how we ever got so unamazed,
but the amazing thing is: Even now
Jesus speaks the poetry of God.
Even now we can touch the hem
of his robe and be healed.
Even now we can share our bread
and our wine with a starving world.
Even now, God the Poet pours grace
upon our heads like snow on snow on snow.
Even now we can be amazed!

West Texas Pilgrimage

Trina Zelle

I drive through country once only visited
in childhood dreams. But now, awake, I move
through its barren landscape to an uncertain
future, finding brief comfort in the clean scent
of creosote released by a sudden downpour.

I fast approach then pass places in the road
where trees overhang their shaggy heads.
Years ago they must have offered the promise
of shelter to other travelers who rarely went
further in a day than their eyes were able to see

and although I do not stop, they reassure
me too, their presence saying that water
is near. The fleeting drone of cicadas
that I hear when I slow down also testifies
to life no less real for its disguise.

And doesn't all our journeying come down
to this ancient search for hidden water
and the discovery that what we seek
sustains us in our seeking? Our travels
cannot end until we learn these truths

that each time we drink or pour, we worship
that our journey is worship, and its end too
when finally, finally, we give ourselves over
to what we have sought and feared for so long
and in that drowning are at last reborn.

Notes

THE SITUATION IS HOPELESS BUT NOT SERIOUS

1. I am indebted to many of my colleagues in the American Association for Marriage and Family Therapy for ideas that I have incorporated in this essay. First, a thanks to Paul Watzlawick, Ph.D., the title of whose book I have used and who has expressed in writings and seminars how many people make themselves unnecessarily unhappy by seeking false goals and engaging in unproductive behavior. I have learned from many others in my profession how to help married couples solve some of their common problems using helpful techniques and applying Christian principles for spiritual assistance. I have tried to share some of these ideas in this essay.

2. Paul Watzlawick, *The Situation Is Hopeless, but Not Serious (The Pursuit of Unhappiness)* (New York: W. W. Norton and Co., 1983).

3. Albert Ellis, "Outcome of Employing Three Techniques of Psychotherapy," *Journal of Clinical Psychology* 23 (1957): 344–50.

4. Watzlawick, *Situation Is Hopeless,* 31.

5. Reinhold Neibuhr, *Pious and Secular America* (New York: Charles Scribner and Sons, 1958), 13.

SAINTS AND WRITERS: ON DOING ONE'S WORK IN HIDING

1. See L. Gregory Jones and Stephanie Paulsell, eds., *The Scope of Our Art: The Vocation of the Theological Teacher* (Grand Rapids: Eerdmans, 2002), 17–31.

2. Brenda Ueland, *If You Want to Write* (St. Paul, Minn.: Graywolf Press, 1987), 50.

3. James A. Walsh and George A. Maloney, eds., *The Pursuit of Wisdom and Other Works, by the Author of the Cloud of Unknowing* (New York: Paulist Press, 1988), 236.

4. John Updike, *Self-Consciousness: Memoirs* (New York: A. A. Knopf, 1989), 252.

5. "He who strives for dispassion [*apatheia*] and for God considers lost any day on which he was not criticized." John Climacus, *The Ladder of Divine Ascent*, trans., Colm Luibheid and Norman Russell (New York: Paulist Press, 1982), 120.

6. Natalie Goldberg, *Writing Down the Bones* (Boston: Shambhala Publications, 1986), 57–58.

7. Brenda Maddox, *Nora: The Real Life of Molly Bloom* (New York: Houghton Mifflin, 1988). Quoted in *Newsweek*, June 20, 1988, 64.

8. Admittedly the process of accepting criticism isn't easy. Anne Lamott shares the lament of all writers when she says, "A critic is someone who comes onto the battlefield after the battle is over and shoots the wounded." See *Bird by Bird: Some Instructions on Writing and Life* (New York: Anchor Books, 1995), 142.

9. William Butler Yeats, "Vacillation," in *The Collected Works of W. B. Yeats*, ed., Richard J. Finneran (New York: Scribner, 1997), vol. 1, 255.

10. See Belden C. Lane, "Desert Attentiveness, Desert Indifference: Counter-Cultural Spirituality in the Desert Fathers and Mothers," *Cross Currents* 44:2 (summer, 1994), 193–206, and Thich Nhat Hanh, *The Miracle of Mindfulness* (Boston: Beacon Press, 1987).

11. Mihaly Csikszentmihalyi, *Flow: The Psychology of Optimal Experience* (New York: Harper & Row, 1990).

12. *The Sayings of the Desert Fathers*, trans., Benedicta Ward (Kalamazoo, Mich.: Cistercian Publications, 1984), 211, 244.

13. André Schwarz-Bart, *The Last of the Just*, trans., Stephen Becker (New York: Atheneum, 1961), 5.

14. See C. E. Bosworth, E. Van Donzel, B. Lewis, and Ch. Pellat, eds., *The Encyclopedia of Islam* (Leiden: E. J. Brill), 1986, vol. 5, 543–46.

15. Rainer Marie Rilke, *Letters to a Young Poet*, trans., M. D. Herter Norton (New York: W. W. Norton, 1962), 18–19.

16. Frederick Buechner says, "Nothing is harder to make real than holiness." See William Zinsser, ed., *Spiritual Quests: The Art and Craft of Religious Writing* (New York: Quality Paperback Book Club, 1988), 119.

17. Karl Barth, *Church Dogmatics*, I/1, 188.

18. See *The Journals of Thomas Merton*, ed., Patrick Hart (San Francisco: HarperCollins, 1996–98), 7 vols; Michael Ford, *Wounded Prophet:*

A Portrait of Henri J. M. Nouwen (New York: Doubleday, 1999); Frederick Buechner, *Telling Secrets* (San Francisco: HarperCollins, 1991); and Kathleen Norris, *Amazing Grace: A Vocabulary of Faith* (New York: Riverhead Books, 1998).

19. Merton translated these words from a letter received from Sidi Abdeslam, February 14, 1967. See Michael Mott, *The Seven Mountains of Thomas Merton* (Boston: Houghton Mifflin, 1984), 468.

20. Herbert hid the words from that verse diagonally in his poem. See *George Herbert: The Country Parson, The Temple*, ed., John N. Wall (New York: Paulist Press, 1981), 203.

21. Julian wrote, "But God forbid that you should say or assume that I am a teacher, for that is not and never was my intention; for I am a woman, ignorant, weak and frail. But I know that what I am saying I have received by the revelation of him who is the sovereign teacher." Edmund Colledge and James Walsh, eds., *Julian of Norwich: Showings* (New York: Paulist Press, 1978), Short Text Chapter 6, p. 135.

22. "They laugh at him because he tries to grasp the truth about God in a book of Dogmatics," quipped Barth. "They laugh at the fact that volume follows volume and each is thicker than the previous one. . . . And they laugh about the men who write so much about Karl Barth instead of writing about the things he is trying to write about." Quoted in Georges Casalis, *Portrait of Karl Barth* (Garden City, N.Y.: Doubleday, 1963), 3.

23. See Diane Ackerman, "O Muse! You Do Make Things Difficult!" *New York Times Book Review*, November 12, 1989), 1, 56–57. Jacques Barzun says that, "The hopelessly stuck would find it expensive but worth it to hire a gunman to pound on the door and threaten death as a spur to composition. Ideas would come thick and fast and yet be sorted out with wonderful clarity in that final message to one's literary executors." *On Writing, Editing, and Publishing* (Chicago: University of Chicago Press, 1971), 6–7.

24. Lamott, *Bird by Bird*, xxvi.

WHY DO YOU WRITE FOR CHILDREN?

1. Flannery O'Connor, *Mystery and Manners* (New York: Farrar, Straus and Giroux, 1979), 81.

2. Ibid.

3. Barry Lopez, "Story at Anaktuvak Pass," *Harper's*, December 1998, 52.

4. Sven Birketts, *The Gutenberg Elegies: The Fate of Reading in an Electronic Age* (New York: Fawcett Columbine, 1994).

WE ARE EARTHLINGS

1. William F. Bade, *The Life and Letters of John Muir* (New York: Houghton Mifflin Press, 1924).

2. *The Bergen Record*, Feb. 18, 1993.

3. James Weldon Johnson, *God's Trombones: Seven Negro Sermons in Verse*, in *The Selected Writings of James Weldon Johnson* (New York: Oxford University Press, 1995).

4. As cited in William Cronon, *Changes in the Land: Indians, Colonists, and the Ecology of New England* (New York: Hill and Wang Publishers, 1984).

5. Rachel Carson, *Silent Spring* (New York: Mariner Books, 2002).

6. Bill McKibben, *The End of Nature* (New York: Random House, 1989).

7. Aldo Leopold, *A Sand County Almanac* (New York: Oxford University Press, 2002).

Contributors

John Barden currently serves as pastor of First Presbyterian Church in Fulton, Missouri. His stories first appeared in print almost twenty years ago in the student literary journal of the University of the South. After receiving his bachelor's degree in religion, he earned a master of divinity from Austin Presbyterian Theological Seminary and a doctor of ministry from McCormick Theological Seminary. His thesis, a collection of new Appalachian folktales for preaching, earned the John Randall Hunt Prize.

Doris Betts is the author of nine novels and short story collections, including *Souls Raised from the Dead*, which the New York Times named as one of the best twenty books of 1994. Her other books include *The Sharp Teeth of Love*, *The Astronomer and Other Stories*, *Tall House in the Winter*, *The Scarlet Thread*, and *Beast of the Southern Wild and Other Stories*. She is professor emerita of English at the University of North Carolina–Chapel Hill. She is also a recipient of the Presbyterian Writers Guild Distinguished Writer Award (1998).

Donna Blackstock is a writer, editor, and educator who operates a small business called Words' Worth that provides publication services for people and organizations. She worked for more than twenty years in the development, editing, and publishing of curriculum materials for the PC(USA).

Kathleen Long Bostrom is an ordained minister in the PC(USA). She and her husband serve as copastors of the Wildwood Presbyterian Church near Chicago. She is the author of over a dozen books for children, including *Song of Creation*, *The Snake in the Grass*, and *Green Plagues and Lamb* (Westminster John Knox Press). She is currently president of the Presbyterian Writers Guild. Kathy earned a master of arts and master of divinity from Princeton Theological Seminary, and a doctor of ministry in preaching from McCormick Theological Seminary.

Patricia Bulko has taught piano, worked as a librarian, and served as an emergency medical technician in Vassar, Michigan. She is married and has two grown sons, three grandsons, and two daughters-in-law. She has just started writing her first novel, a mystery.

Stephen Doughty is an ordained minister in the PC(USA). He served twenty-three years as pastor and ten as executive presbyter for the Presbytery of Lake Michigan. He is the author of three books and numerous essays. His fourth book, on integrity and spiritual leadership, will be published in 2004 by Upper Room.

Joan Ellison has published four collections of poetry and is also a prize-winning poet in the West Virginia Poetry Society. She has taught in the public schools of West Virginia and Kentucky and is married to a Presbyterian minister. She is an ordained elder in the PC(USA).

Elsie Gilmore is a high school teacher of literature and writing, and has taught English as a second language. She also taught for a year in China. She is a wife and the mother of four adult children, and is an active member of Baraboo Presbyterian Church.

George W. Gunn is a native of West Virginia and a graduate of Davidson College and Louisville Seminary. He has served as a campus minister and was a founder and early president of the National Campus Ministry Association. His writings have appeared in journals and periodicals, and he was a contributor to the *Encyclopedia of Religion in the South*. His paraphrases of 1 Corinthians 13 were published in 2001 under the title *Love's Letters, a Poetic Book of Confessions*. He lives and writes from his home in Banner Elk, North Carolina.

Jeanette Hardage is a freelance writer living by a swamp in South Carolina with her husband of fifty-four years and a fat cat. Her work has appeared in the *International Bulletin of Missionary Research*, *Charleston Post and Courier*, *Mars Hill Review*, *Christian Science Monitor*, and several other publications.

James R. Hine has served as pastor to churches in Indiana, Illinois, and Arizona. He was granted the Distinguished Alumni Award by McCormick Theological Seminary in 1993 and the Lifetime Achievement Award from the University of Arizona in 2001.

Vic Jameson has served in the U.S. Army, worked as a reporter for the *Hobbs Daily Sun*, and was on staff of the Presbyterian Office of Information in New York City. In 1983 he became editor of *Presbyterian Survey*, and continued until he retired in 1991. He has also served as editor of *These Days*, a multidenominational devotional magazine. His writing includes plays, lyrics for musicals, and two books, *Bull at a New Gate* and *Dear Hearts: Conversations with Presbyterians*. He was awarded the Distinguished Writer Award from the Presbyterian Writers Guild in 1992.

J. Marshall Jenkins is director of counseling at Berry College and a psychologist in private practice in Rome, Georgia. He received his doctor of philosophy in counseling psychology from the University of North Carolina at Chapel Hill in 1986 and his bachelor of arts in philosophy from Davidson College in 1980. He wrote *A Wakeful Faith: Spiritual Practice in the Real World* (Upper Room, 2000) and *The Ancient Laugh of God: Divine Encounters in Unlikely Places* (Westminster John Knox Press, 1994). He has published articles in *The Christian Century*, *Lectionary Homiletics*, and *The Pastoral Forum*. He lives in Rome, Georgia, with his wife, Sharon, and his son, Philip.

Belden C. Lane is a Presbyterian theologian teaching on a Jesuit faculty of theology in the department of theological studies at Saint Louis University. His books include *The Solace of Fierce Landscapes* and *Landscapes of the Sacred*. He has written several articles, most recently in *Spiritus: A Journal of Christian Spirituality* and *Church History*.

Aminta Marks holds degrees from Wilson College and Princeton Theological Seminary. She is a writer, painter, mother, and grandmother of six. She is married to Old Testament scholar and Princeton University professor John Marks.

Derek Maul is a freelance writer and teacher living in the greater Tampa, Florida, area. His column, "Reading

Between the Lines," is a weekly feature in several newspapers. His devotional writing appears frequently in *These Days* and *The Upper Room*, and he is a regular contributor to *Presbyterians Today*. His wife, Rebekah, is a Presbyterian pastor, and they have two children.

Michael McCormack holds a master of divinity from Louisville Presbyterian Seminary. Greatly influenced by the poetry of the Bible and contemporary poets such as Billy Collins, Michael tries to make the Christian life intersect the world through his writing.

George R. Pasley has been pastor at Garnett and Miami Presbyterian Churches, two small congregations in rural Kansas, for five years. Prior to entering the ministry, he was a shepherd and professional sheep-shearer. His poetry has been published in several magazines, including *Presbyterian Outlook* and *Journal of Christian Nursing*.

Katherine Paterson is the author of more than thirty books, including fourteen novels for young people, and has twice won both the Newbery Medal and the National Book Award. Her books have been published in twenty-six languages, and she is the 1998 recipient of the distinguished international award for children's literature, the Hans Christian Andersen Medal. She is also a recipient of the Presbyterian Writers Guild's Distinguished Writer Award (1989). *The Invisible Child*, a collection of essays on reading and writing for children, was published in 2001. Her most recent novel, published in 2002, is *The Same Stuff as Stars*.

John C. Purdy is an honorably retired minister of the PC(USA). After twelve years as a pastor in Wisconsin, he became curriculum editor for the United Presbyterian Church (U.S.A.) and the PC(USA). After twenty-six years in curriculum editing, he retired to the life of a freelance writer. He has written several books, including *Parables at Work*.

J. Barrie Shepherd is a popular speaker and writer in the PC(USA). He is the author of several books, including *Diary of Daily Prayer*, *A Child Is Born*, *Pilgrim's Way*, and *Praying the Psalms* (Westminster John Knox Press).

Martha Evans Sparks is a member of Trinity Avenue Presbyterian Church in Durham, North Carolina, where she was the first woman elected elder. She has degrees in journalism, psychology, and library science, and has published numerous articles in newspaper and religious and professional journals.

David Steele was a pastor in the PC(USA) and a popular writer and speaker. For years he had a regular column in *Presbyterian Outlook*, and authored several books, including *Slow Down*, *Moses*, and *The Next Voice You Hear*. David passed away in 2001. The Presbyterian Writers Guild recently named their Distinguished Writer Award in his memory.

Eva Stimson is editor of *Presbyterians Today*. She has served on the staff of the magazine since 1984, becoming editor in 1997. She holds a master of arts in Christian education from the Presbyterian School of Christian Education and a master of arts in English from Georgia State University. She is married to Jerry Van Marter, and they are parents of eleven-year-old twins. She is an ordained elder at Crescent Hill Presbyterian Church in Louisville, Kentucky.

Bill Tammeus was the winner of the 2003 Distinguished Writer Award from the Presbyterian Writers Guild. He has worked in journalism his entire career, and was a member of the staff of the *Kansas City Star* that won the Pulitzer Prize for local reporting in 1982. His column has been syndicated nationwide, and he has received numerous awards for his writing. His book, *A Gift of Meaning*, was published in 2001.

Jerry L. Van Marter is a lifelong Presbyterian and ordained minister. He has been a pastor, a member of the staff of the Synod of the Pacific, and, since 1988, a writer for the *Presbyterian News Service*. He is married to Eva Stimson, editor of *Presbyterians Today*, and they have eleven-year-old twins.

Louis B. Weeks is president and professor of historical theology at Union Theological Seminary–Presbyterian School of Christian Education in Richmond, Virginia. He was previously a professor and dean at Louisville Presbyterian Theological Seminary for many years. An ordained minister in the Presbyterian Church (U.S.A.), he served congregations in North Carolina and Kentucky and served on numerous committees of the General Assembly. He has also served on the board of directors for the Louisville Institute for the Study of Protestantism and American Culture, as well as on the editorial board of *Interpretation*. Weeks is the author of numerous articles, case-studies, and books, including *The Presbyterian Source: Bible Words That Shape a Faith* (Westminster John Knox Press, 1990), *To Be a Presbyterian* (Westminster John Knox Press, 1983), and was coauthor of *Vital Signs: The Promise of Mainstream Protestantism*.

Ann Weems is a popular writer, poet, speaker, liturgist, and seminar leader. She is the author of several books, including *Kneeling in Bethlehem*, *Kneeling in Jerusalem*, *Putting the Amazing Back in Grace*, and *Psalms of Lament* (Westminster John Knox Press). She is coeditor of *Faith in Words*. She is also a recipient of the Presbyterian Writers Guild's Distinguished Writer Award (1996).

Trina Zelle, an ordained Presbyterian minister, has been involved in parish ministry and advocacy work in settings as diverse as rural Connecticut, urban Honolulu, and the border region of New Mexico and Texas. She is the author of two books and several articles and poems.